The Coopbook: Wholesome Meals for your Flock, and More!
Copyright © 2023 by Nancy Simat

All rights reserved. No part of this publication may be reproduced, distributed, or transmitted in any form or by any means, including photocopying, recording, or other electronic or mechanical methods, without the prior written permission of the publisher, except in the case of brief quotations embodied in critical reviews and certain other noncommercial uses permitted by copyright law.

Published by The Canary Agency. www.canaryagency.com

For permission requests, write to the author, addressed "Attention: Permissions Coordinator," at Njsimat@gmail.com

Unless otherwise noted, Photography is by the Author, by courtesy of Silkie Acres, and/or used under a license of Canva, and Midjourney.

Disclaimer:
The authors of this book are not veterinarians or avian health professionals. The content provided, including all recipes and advice, is intended for informational purposes only and should not be considered as professional veterinary advice, diagnosis, or treatment. While every effort has been made to ensure the accuracy and effectiveness of the information presented in this book, we cannot guarantee that every chicken will react positively to the recipes and suggestions provided.
Every bird's health, needs, and potential allergies are unique. Before introducing any new food or making changes to your chicken's diet, it is essential to consult with a qualified veterinarian or avian health specialist, especially if your bird shows signs of distress, illness, or allergic reactions.
By choosing to use the recipes and advice contained in this book, you accept all risks and responsibilities. The authors and publishers expressly disclaim any liability arising from the use or application of the information contained herein.

LCCN:
ISBN: 978-1-7379030-2-4 HC
ISBN: 978-1-7379030-4-8 (ebook)
ISBN: 978-1-7379030-3-1 Paperback

THE COOPBOOK

Wholesome Recipes for your Flock and More!

Created By: Author N. J. Simat & Silkie Acre's Eva Carver

To all our feathered friends
we've lost along the way,

You taught us about the cycles of life
and the value in each day,

Your feathers may've returned to Earth,
but you fly on,
forever in our hearts.

	Introduction	
1	The Staples	5
2	Recipes by Season	19
3	Recipes by Month	46
4	Recipes for Support	61
5	Love Spells	92
6	Sprouts	99
7	Best Practices & Precautions	107
	Harmful Foods and Plants	108
8	Bonus Material and Charts	118
	Recipe Index	132
	Ingredient Benefit Indexes	136
	Glossary	150

Welcome to The Coopbook

A Cookbook of Wholesome Recipes for Your Flock.

Introduction

Chickens have been our companions throughout history; providing entertainment, companionship, and let's not forget the reward of fresh, home-laid eggs. They've inspired folklore, art, literature, and mascots, securing a special place in the hearts of millions. Whether you're an experienced chicken keeper or just beginning your journey, this cookbook offers a range of nutritious and delectable recipes that will have your chickens clucking with delight. But, this unique culinary collection is more than just a cookbook, it's cluck-full of helpful information, addresses common questions and concerns, and offers plenty of supplementary resources.

Keeping chickens comes with its responsibilities, a significant part of which involves understanding their dietary needs. Chickens are omnivorous, with a diverse palate that includes grains, insects, vegetables, and even small rodents and lizards at times. Their natural diet is a testament to their adaptability and resourcefulness. As responsible chicken keepers, we must ensure their diet is balanced and nutritious. A nutrient-deficient diet can lead to poor health, decreased egg production, increased susceptibility to diseases, or even behavioral issues.

Throughout the pages, we'll delve into the fascinating culinary world of our feathered friends. From straightforward homemade feeds to seasonal delicacies, we've meticulously curated a selection that covers a spectrum of flavors, textures, and nutrients. Our goal is to equip you with a variety of recipes that not only meet the nutritional needs of your chickens but also bring enrichment and wellness to their daily meals.

We'll explore their dietary needs, share recipes that meet these requirements, and introduce fun and tasty treats for special rewards and occasions. Moreover, we will address common pitfalls and health issues, discuss some foods chickens should avoid, and provide some tried and true best practices.

If you're reading this book then we don't have to tell you that raising chickens extends beyond mere amusement. It's a journey that deepens our connection to nature, promotes responsibility, sustainable living, and provides valuable learning opportunities for both adults and children. Chickens are more than just farm animals, they are intelligent beings with distinct personalities and refined tastes. Furthermore, we recognize, from personal experience, that chickens are not just creatures of habit but also beings of curiosity. They relish exploration, pecking, and the discovery of new flavors. That's why we've incorporated recipes that will bring joy and a unique quality to your feeding times. Whether it's a gourmet snack or a holiday banquet, these recipes will enable you to create unforgettable memories for your flock.

So, fellow poultry enthusiasts, don your aprons and embark on this culinary journey with us. Let's explore diverse flavors, nourish our chickens, and deepen our connection with these extraordinary creatures. Let's start cooking!

| 1.1 Essential Components of a Balanced Feed | 1.2 Homemade Feeds | 1.3 Supplemental Greens |

CHAPTER 1 THE STAPLES

In this chapter, we'll explore the foundation of a nutritious diet. We'll guide you through creating a simple homemade chicken feed using a variety of grains, legumes, and vegetables. By preparing these wholesome feeds, you can help your chickens receive the essential nutrients they need for optimal health and vitality. As any seasoned chicken keeper would attest, the foundation of good care lies in the daily diet you offer them.

1.1 Essential Components of a Balanced Diet

Grains:

Grains such as corn, oats, and wheat are excellent sources of energy for your chickens. They are rich in carbohydrates, which chickens need for daily activities and to maintain body heat. However, while grains are essential, they should not constitute the entirety of your chicken's diet, as they are not sufficiently high in other vital nutrients like proteins and fat.

Seeds & Legumes:

Black sunflower seeds and flaxseeds are excellent sources of essential fats, which are crucial for maintaining a healthy and consistent body composition in chickens, as well as supporting regular egg laying. On the other hand, legumes, including lentils, peas, and soybeans, are rich in protein. This vital nutrient plays a key role in promoting growth, egg production, and overall health in chickens. Among these legumes, cooked soybeans are frequently used in chicken feed due to their high protein content. However, it's important to note that raw or undercooked beans should never be given to chickens. This is because they contain harmful toxins, which are neutralized through the cooking process.

The Greens:

Vegetables are essential to a chicken's diet, offering crucial vitamins and minerals. Chickens have quite a varied taste palette when it comes to vegetables, showing a marked preference for leafy greens such as arugula, butter lettuce, and kale, and providing these greens raw guarantees a nutritious and fresh meal for the chickens. However, it's imperative to ensure that these vegetables are not only clean but also free from pesticides or harmful chemicals to safeguard the chickens' health. In addition to vegetables, chickens also benefit immensely from eating grass. The act of foraging in the grass not only stimulates their natural behavior but also provides an extra source of dietary fiber, aiding in digestion and potentially helping to control internal parasites. A note on Iceburg lettuce, because of its limited nutritional value, it should only be offered in moderation.

1.2 Homemade Feeds

Now, let's begin the process of creating our homemade chicken feeds. Not only can this be a more cost-effective approach, but it also gives you control over what goes into your chicken's diet, ensuring that it's fresh, wholesome, and free of unnecessary additives. Creating a homemade feed is an enriching experience for the whole family. After all, there's something immensely satisfying about watching your chickens happily pecking away at the nutritious meal you've prepared for them! On the following pages, we've compiled a variety of simple recipes for homemade feeds, starting from a basic grain mix to more varied blends incorporating legumes and vegetables. Each recipe will include a list of ingredients, clear instructions, and the benefits each feed provides to your flock.

1. Basic Homemade Chicken Feed

 Flock of 10   15 minutes

INGREDIENTS
8 Cups whole corn
6 Cups whole raw oats
2 Cups Black-Oil Sunflower Seeds
2 Cups of Flax Seeds
1 Cup of Millet
(Optional)
1 container red pepper flakes
1/2 of a finely chopped and dehydrated garlic bulb

DIRECTIONS

1. Combine all ingredients in a large container and mix them well.
2. Use a grain grinder or a high-powered blender to partially grind the mixture. This step is optional, but grinding can make it easier for the chickens to digest the feed. Be careful not to over-grind, as a coarse mix is much better than a fine powder because the coarse mixture acts as a grit for digestion.
3. Store the feed in a cool, dry place, ideally in a rodent-proof container.
4. Remember to supplement this feed with calcium, especially for laying hens. You can do this by providing crushed oyster shells in a separate feeder. Also, greens and other vegetable scraps can provide additional nutrients and variety.
5. (optional) To dehydrate garlic, remove the papery skin from the garlic cloves and mince the garlic. Preheat your oven to the lowest temperature setting (usually around 150°F) and place the garlic on a baking sheet lined with parchment paper or a silicone mat. Dry the garlic for several hours until it becomes crispy.

*Please note that this is a basic recipe, and it might need to be adjusted depending on the specific needs of your chickens, ie. the amount of free ranging time, their life stage (chicks, layers, or old birds), and/or the availability of certain ingredients in your area. Always consult with a poultry nutrition expert or veterinarian before completely switching to a homemade diet to ensure that all nutritional needs of your chickens are being met.

BENEFITS:

This feed is great for a flock that gets plenty of free-ranging time and just needs a supplementary feed. The oats are high in fiber and provide a good balance of carbohydrates and protein, they also contain essential minerals like manganese, selenium, and zinc. The sunflower seeds and flaxseeds provide healthy fats. The Millet its high protein content can be especially beneficial for laying hens, which require additional protein for egg production. Moreover, millet (and corn) is a good source of carbohydrates, which can provide energy for the chickens

Optional Ingredients: Red pepper flakes are often added to chicken feed for the active component of Capsaicin-chickens are not sensitive to the heat from the peppers-which is believed to act as a natural anti-parasitic, stimulate circulation, and provide antioxidants that will contribute to an overall healthy hen. Similarly, garlic is valued for its natural antibacterial and antiviral properties that can support chickens' immune systems.

> **NOTES**
> Monitor your chickens' consumption and adjust the feed quantities as needed to prevent over-eating or waste, and always make sure your flock has access to clean water
> **See the Body Condition chart in Chapter 7 p.112**

2. The Overachiever

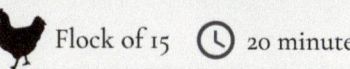 Flock of 15   ⏱ 20 minutes

INGREDIENTS

4 cups of Whole Corn
3 cups of Wheat
2 cups of Oats
1 cup of Sunflower Seeds
1 cup of dried Peas
1 cup of dried Lentils
1/2 cup of Flaxseeds
1/4 cup of Food Grade Kelp Meal
1/4 cup of FOOD GRADE Diatomaceous Earth*

DIRECTIONS

1. Mix all the ingredients together in a large container until well combined.
2. Use a grain grinder or a high-powered blender to partially grind the mixture. This step is optional, but grinding can make it easier for the chickens to digest the feed. Be careful not to over-grind, as a coarse mix is much better than a fine powder because the coarse mixture acts as a grit for digestion.
3. Store the feed in a cool, dry place to prevent it from going bad. A locking container is ideal to keep out pests.
4. Feed your chickens this mixture as their main diet. The exact amount will depend on the size and breed of your chickens, but generally, an adult chicken will eat about 1/4 to 1/3 cup of feed per day.

> **NOTES**
> Kelp Meal and Whole Wheat can be found at Local Feed Stores, Online Retailers, Garden Supply, Farm Supply, Pet Supply Stores, and Health Food Stores.

BENEFITS:

This homemade chicken feed recipe is balanced and nutritious, providing a variety of different nutrients that chickens need to stay healthy. The whole grains provide energy and fiber. Oats are also high in fiber and provide a good balance of carbohydrates and protein; they also contain essential minerals like manganese, selenium, and zinc. The sunflower seeds and flaxseeds provide healthy fats, and the peas and lentils provide much-needed protein. The kelp meal adds a boost of vitamins and minerals.

*(DE) is often used as a supplement in chicken feed due to its potential health benefits. It is believed by many that DE is a natural anti-parasitic. The microscopic sharp edges of DE can cut through the exoskeletons of parasites, causing them to dehydrate and die. It's typically recommended to add about 2% of the total feed weight and is important to note that you must always use food-grade DE when adding it to chicken feed or using it around your chickens. Also never pour DE out in an enclosed space where your birds are existing, the dust can irritate their respiratory systems.

3. Supplemental Salad

 Flock of 15   5 minutes

INGREDIENTS

4 cups chopped arugula
2 cups chopped kale
2 cups chopped Swiss chard
1 cup of green peas
(optional)
1 cup cherry tomatoes

A golden egg! This means that the recipe can be shared with the flock *and* the family!

DIRECTIONS

1. Be sure to chop all greens very well. Long or stringy pieces can cause crop impaction.
2. Combine all ingredients in a bowl.
3. Serve the leafy green medley as a nutritious supplement to your chickens' diet, alongside any homemade feed.
4. Introduce the greens gradually, in small amounts to allow their digestive systems to adjust.

NOTES

These ingredients grow well in the fall and winter, when the grass' nutrition is lacking.
TIP: Grow and Harvest fresh leafy greens (and other chicken ingredients) from your own "Chicken-Kitchen" garden, or purchase organic varieties from a trusted source.
See Chicken Kitchen Garden in Ch. 8's Bonus Material

BENEFITS:

Arugula, kale, and Swiss chard are leafy greens rich in vitamins A, C, and K, as well as calcium and other minerals, which can enhance overall health, and immunity, and contribute to robust bones and eggshells in chickens. Swiss chard provides fiber, aiding digestion. Cherry tomatoes are acidic, good for crop health, and high in vitamins A and C, potassium, and the antioxidant lycopene.

However, tomatoes should be given in moderation, fully ripe, and without any of their green parts to avoid solanine, which can harm chickens.

4. Vegetable Mash-up

 Flock of 10   45 minutes

INGREDIENTS

2 cups grated carrots

2 cup finely chopped zucchini

2-3 sweet potatoes

1 butternut squash

1/4 of chopped Parsley

1/2 cup of millet

> If you want to add salt/sugar to a dish for your family, just make sure to add it after the chickens get their portion.

DIRECTIONS

1. Cube sweet potatoes and butternut squash before tossing them into boiling water for 30 minutes or until tender.
2. **Remove the skin of the sweet potatoes.**
3. Combine the sweet potatoes, butternut squash, grated carrots, and zucchini in a food processor or a blender. Blend until smooth.
4. Sprinkle the millet and chopped parsley on top.
5. Let cool, then serve.

NOTES

Introduce gradually to allow your chickens to adjust to new flavors and textures. You can also prepare 12 batches ahead of time without the millet and freeze in non-BPA containers, and start each month with a blast of nutrients!

BENEFITS:

Chickens thrive on a varied diet, and ingredients like grated carrots, sweet potatoes, finely chopped zucchini, butternut squash, parsley, and millet are not just treats but nutritional powerhouses. Carrots, rich in vitamin A, play a pivotal role in enhancing eye health and fortifying immunity. Zucchini, brimming with vitamins C, B6, potassium, and magnesium, nurtures cellular functions and strengthens the immune system. Sweet potatoes and parsley work in tandem to boost overall health. Butternut squash, laden with vitamins A and C, fiber, potassium, and magnesium, not only aids digestion and immunity but its seeds can also act as a natural anti parasitic. Then there's millet, a crunchy delight for chickens. This nutritious grain is a good protein source, promoting feather vibrancy and egg production, while its B vitamins energize our feathered friends.

Chapter 2

Seasonal Feasts

In this chapter, we'll explore the rhythm of synergistic recipes for your chickens. By incorporating fresh and seasonal ingredients into their diet, you can provide additional nutrients and flavors that celebrate the changing seasons and stay in harmony with nature.

Nutritious Delights with Seasonal Ingredients

Seasons ebb and flow, each bringing its unique offerings. Just as our menus change to embrace the bounties of different seasons, our chickens will also appreciate a diverse rotation of seasonal fare. This practice of seasonal feeding not only adds an exciting variety to their diets but also ensures that they enjoy a broad spectrum of nutrients throughout the year. From hearty autumn dishes to vibrant spring salads, these recipes will nourish your chickens while embracing the beauty of nature's bounty.

SPRING

In the spring, the world awakens from its winter slumber and brings abundance in the form of fresh greens and insects. Your flock will be eager for the new growth all around them, as it is brimming with nutrients.

5. Spring-Green Salad Bar

FLOCK OF 10 10 MIN

A celebration of this season's freshest produce – a delightful mix of leafy greens and herbs that your chickens will love. With the increased insect activity, your chickens will naturally get a rich supply of protein during this time.

Ingredients

To customize your mix of herbs, flowers, & greens, **see Index p. 136, 146**

Select 3 Fresh herbs (such as parsley, oregano, basil, and/or mint)

Select 2 Edible flowers (such as nasturtiums and marigold petals)

And Select 2 Spring greens (such as arugula and butter lettuce)

Directions

1. Wash and dry the spring greens, herbs, and edible flowers thoroughly.
2. Tear greens into small, bite-sized pieces and place them in a salad bowl.
3. Finely chop the fresh herbs and sprinkle them over the greens.
4. Gently mix the ingredients to combine them evenly and arrange the edible flowers on top of the salad, before serving.

BENEFITS:

The leafy greens are a good source of vitamins A, K, some vitamin C, and folate. Parsley is rich in vitamins and antioxidants, supports the immune system, and may aid in egg production. Oregano is known for its antibacterial and antiviral properties. Basil is packed with vitamins and antioxidants and is thought to promote respiratory health due to its anti-inflammatory and antibacterial properties. Mint is known for its cooling effects, is a source of vitamins and iron, and is used for its insect-repelling properties and has the potential to lower body temperature on hot days. Nasturtiums, where the whole plant is safe for chickens, are rich in vitamin C, have natural antibiotic properties, and are believed to deter pests. Marigold petals are believed to enhance egg yolk color and have antioxidant properties.

6. Melon Medley!

FLOCK OF 10   15 MIN

Simplicity is key here!

Ingredients

1 Cantaloupe

1 Honey Dew Melon

1 Watermelon

1 Tablespoon Of Probiotics (Probios is our preferred brand)

Directions

1. Start by cubing the cantaloupe, honey dew melon, and watermelon.
2. Add the cubed melons to a large mixing bowl.
3. Sprinkle a generous amount of Probios (or your preferred brand of probiotics) over the melons.
4. Toss the melons to evenly distribute the probiotics.
5. Once everything is well mixed, serve to your flock.

BENEFITS:

Melons, including watermelon and cantaloupe, are not only a hydrating treat for chickens due to their approximately 90% water content, but also a vital source of refreshment during the intense heat of summer. These fruits are packed with essential nutrients such as vitamins A, C, E, and B-vitamins, in addition to minerals like potassium and magnesium. The fiber content of melons is beneficial for gut health, and given their low-calorie nature, they pose minimal risk of contributing to weight gain. Serving melons can also engage chickens, potentially curbing detrimental behaviors like feather pecking.

Some suggest that melon seeds might harbor anti-parasitic properties due to the presence of cucurbitacin, but there isn't strong scientific evidence to back this up. Hence, standard deworming procedures should remain a priority. While melons can be an enjoyable treat, they shouldn't replace main dietary staples, as overconsumption may lead to digestive issues or nutrient imbalances.

It's important to promptly remove any uneaten melon pieces to avert bacterial and mold growth.

SUMMER

Underneath the sun's warm glow,
Near the barn, where breezes blow.

Feathers ruffle in the light,
Clucking softly—sweet delight.

Amidst summer's golden reign,
Chickens peck in fields of green.

-NJ. SIMAT

7. Summer Berry Blast!

FLOCK OF 15   15 MIN

As the heat of summer takes hold, the 'Summer Berry Blast' provides a cooling treat. A mix of strawberries, blueberries, and raspberries, this recipe not only offers a tasty snack but also helps to keep your chickens hydrated. Additionally, always provide cool and fresh water to your flock, checking it regularly for mold or contaminants.

Ingredients

2 LB Unflavored Chobani Greek Yogurt

6 oz Blackberries

6 oz Raspberries

8 oz Blueberries

8 oz sliced Strawberries

Directions

Option 1:

Mix all ingredients together for a fresh and fun summer treat for your flock.

Option 2:

On particularly hot days, blend with ice and serve it as a frozen treat!

BENEFITS:

Greek yogurt, especially the lactose-free variety, is an aid to chickens. It is a rich source of probiotics, proteins, and vitamins, providing a robust defense against the humid environments of summer that can foster mold, bacteria, and parasites.

The Blackberries are teeming with fiber, vitamins, antioxidants, and manganese, contributing to bone development and fortifying the immune system. Raspberries, another wholesome choice, facilitate digestion, strengthen the immune system, and support heart health. Blueberries offer an abundance of iron, zinc, fiber, vitamin C, and vitamin K, equipping chickens to better manage stress and fend off diseases. Even the leaves from blueberry bushes, known for their high antioxidant content, are safe for chickens to consume. Strawberries serve as a nutritious snack, brimming with vitamin C, B9, antioxidants, manganese, and potassium. These nutrients not only aid in metabolism but also foster overall health in chickens. Thus, incorporating such nutrient-rich foods into a chicken's diet can significantly enhance their well-being.

8. Revitalize and Repel, Nesting Box Mix

ALL FLOCK SIZES   5 MIN

These edible herbs and flowers offer more than just dietary benefits. During the height of summer, when flowers are in full bloom and bugs are rampant, your coop might need a refresh. This herbal mix is a great addition, providing a natural way to maintain cleanliness and repel pests.

Ingredients

Calendula (Marigold): It acts as a deterrent for pests.
Chamomile: This herb can calm laying hens.
Cornflower: A potent aid for immunity, use it sparingly as a little goes a long way.
Lavender: Known for its calming effect on laying hens, it also repels pests.
Peppermint: This herb is effective in keeping rodents at bay.
Rose Petals: These add a pleasant aroma to the coop.
Rosemary: A natural pest deterrent.
Spearmint: Another herb that can help keep rodents away.

Directions

1. Gather freshly harvested flowers from the list or purchase some from a store.
2. Next, arrange these flowers in the hens' nesting boxes. OR An alternate method involves drying the flowers before adding them to the nesting boxes.
To do this, hang them up in a well-ventilated area until they're completely dry.
4. Remember, it's not necessary to purchase new herbs every year. For more detailed information on growing your own herbs, refer to our bonus content in Chapter 8.

BENEFITS:

Certain flowers can be a beneficial addition to a chicken's nesting box, or diet, due to their varied properties. For instance, Calendula, also known as Marigold, is recognized for its ability to deter pests, thus maintaining a cleaner nesting environment for chickens. Chamomile is well-regarded for its calming effect on laying hens, potentially enhancing egg production. Cornflower, though only required in small quantities, can contribute to a chicken's immunity, bolstering their resistance against diseases. Lavender, similar to chamomile, helps calm laying hens but also doubles as a pest repellent, ensuring an extra layer of protection for your chickens. Both Peppermint and Spearmint are known to deter rodents, which is crucial for maintaining a secure and hygienic environment for your chickens. Rose petals serve an aesthetic purpose, infusing the coop with a pleasant aroma, thereby improving the overall ambiance. Finally, Rosemary plays a key role as a pest deterrent, similar to Calendula and Lavender, further contributing to a safer and cleaner coop. However, while these flowers offer benefits, they should only serve as a complement to a well-rounded, chicken-specific diet and thorough coop management, not as a replacement for traditional pest control strategies or nutritious chicken feed.

notes

FALL

As the leaves start to fall, it's a reminder that it's time to prepare your livestock for the colder months ahead. This is when you'll start to incorporate more grains into their diet to ensure they maintain their weight and stay healthy through the winter.

9. Oh-My-Gourd Harvest

FLOCK OF 15+   35 MIN

Ingredients

1 small butternut squash, peeled and diced

1 small pumpkin, seeds removed and diced.

2 tablespoons olive oil

1 teaspoon thyme

1 teaspoon rosemary

1/4 cup pumpkin seeds

Directions

1. Preheat your oven to 400°F (200°C).

2. In a mixing bowl, toss the diced butternut squash and pumpkin with olive oil, dried thyme and rosemary ensuring the pieces are well coated.

3. Spread the seasoned squash and pumpkin evenly on a baking sheet.

4. Roast in the preheated oven for 25-30 minutes or until the vegetables are tender and slightly caramelized.

5. Meanwhile, lightly toast the pumpkin seeds in a dry skillet over medium heat for a few minutes until they turn golden and fragrant.

6. sprinkle the pumpkin seeds over the medley.

7. Serve Cool!

BENEFITS:

Pumpkins provide a significant health boost to chickens, thanks to their abundance of vitamins and minerals. These include essential vitamins A and C, potassium, and zinc, all of which contribute to maintaining the chickens' overall health. Some chicken keepers also value pumpkin seeds for their alleged antiparasitic properties, believed to stem from the compound cucurbitacin. Herbs like thyme and rosemary also offer multiple health benefits to chickens. They are rich in essential oils and recognized for their inherent antibacterial and antiparasitic properties. Thyme is particularly revered for supporting respiratory health, which can help mitigate the risk of respiratory infections in chickens. Rosemary, on the other hand, is a powerful antioxidant-rich herb that aids in maintaining the overall health and well-being of the chickens. These beneficial components make pumpkins, thyme, and rosemary valuable additions to a chicken's diet.

10. Autumn's Scratch

FLOCK OF 10   5 MIN

Ingredients

1 Cup Whole Oats

1 Cup Black Sunflower Seeds

1/2 Cup Dried Oregano

1/2 Cup Raisins

1/2 Cup Dried Cranberries

1 Cup Chicken Feed

Directions

1. Combine the whole oats, black sunflower seeds, dried oregano, raisins, dried cranberries, and chicken feed in an airtight container.

2. Mix all the ingredients together until well combined.

3. Serve this mix as a treat for your chickens.

TIP: Cranberries may help control the level of E.Coli bacteria in your chickens. See Cranberries in the ingredient-benefit index for details.

BENEFITS:

Feeding chickens a mix of whole oats, black sunflower seeds, dried oregano, raisins, dried cranberries, and chicken feed can offer an array of health benefits due to the nutrients they collectively provide. Whole oats are a rich source of dietary fiber, which aids digestion and provides chickens with a slow-releasing energy source. The black sunflower seeds are packed with healthy fats and proteins crucial for feather health and overall energy levels. They also contain a high amount of Vitamin E, an important antioxidant. Dried oregano is known for its antimicrobial properties, potentially aiding in the prevention of diseases and promoting good respiratory health. The raisins and dried cranberries offer natural sweetness and are packed with antioxidants and vitamins, especially Vitamin C, which can support the immune system. However, they should be given sparingly due to their sugar content. Lastly, chicken feed is a complete balanced diet for chickens, providing the right mix of protein, carbohydrates, vitamins, and minerals to ensure the chickens' health and productivity. Combined, these ingredients can create a beneficial, nutrient-rich supplemental feed for chickens when offered in moderation and alongside their standard diet.

notes

WINTER

Winter requires careful attention to your livestock's dietary needs. Ensuring that they have enough to eat to maintain body heat is crucial. The sight of your animals, cozy and content in their winter shelters after enjoying their hearty meals, is a testament to your hard work and dedication.

11. Hearty Vegetable Stew

FLOCK OF 15+   35 MIN

Ingredients
Assorted winter vegetables, diced.

(ie. carrots, pumpkin, and SKINNED potatoes)

1 clove of garlic, minced

4 cups vegetable broth (LOW SODIUM)

1 bay leaf

1 teaspoon dried thyme

Directions
1. Add 1/4 a cup of olive oil to a large pot
2. Fill the pot with the diced vegetables, and cook for a few minutes, stirring occasionally.
3. Meanwhile, sauté the minced garlic over medium heat until it becomes fragrant.
4. Pour the vegetable broth into the pot, ensure that the vegetables are fully submerged.
5. Add the garlic, bay leaf, and dried thyme.
6. Bring the stew to a boil, then reduce the heat to low.
7. Let simmer for 30 minutes or until the vegetables are tender.
8. Allow the stew to cool but serve it warm, never hot.

BENEFITS:

When considering the Winter Vegetable Stew's ingredients for chickens, carrots are beneficial as they are rich in vitamins A, K, and C, and fiber--vitamin A being particularly good for vision and immune function. Potatoes, when cooked and without any green parts (due to toxic solanine), provide essential carbohydrates, vitamins, and minerals. Olive oil adds beneficial fats that offer energy, especially vital during colder months, and promote shiny feathers and skin health. Garlic is renowned for its antimicrobial properties and potential to boost immunity; some poultry enthusiasts also believe it can aid in worm control. The vegetable broth, depending on its composition, can provide essential nutrients and hydration, but it's crucial to ensure it lacks onions or excessive salt due to their potential toxicity to chickens. Lastly, herbs like bay leaf and dried thyme can introduce essential oils and antioxidants, which some suggest support respiratory health and can repel pests.

WARNING: Never serve anything wet or have open water in freezing temperatures. The chickens will dip their heads in the liquid and get frostbite, which can be fatal.

12. Coop Comfort Double-Oatmeal

FLOCK OF 15   15 MIN

Ingredients

4 cup oats
1 cup of oatmilk (or water)
1 tablespoon of cinnamon
optional ;
1 sprig of rosemary

Directions

1. In a saucepan, bring the water or oatmilk to a gentle boil.
2. Stir in the oats and reduce the heat to low.
3. Simmer for 5-7 minutes,
4. Stir occasionally until the oats reach a creamy consistency.
5. Remove the oatmeal from the heat and let it cool slightly.
6. Add a tablespoon of cinnamon and rosemary leaves to the oatmeal.
7. Mix well.
8. Serve the warm oatmeal warm, but not hot.

TIP: If the finished product is too runny, you can adjust the consistency of the oatmeal by simply adding more oats—and it does not need to be cooked any further after adding the oats.

BENEFITS:

Oatmeal and cinnamon offer several benefits to chickens during cold winter months. Oatmeal, being a warm and hearty grain, provides essential energy and carbohydrates, helping chickens maintain body temperature and energy levels in cold weather. It's also rich in fiber, which aids in digestion.

On the other hand, cinnamon is believed to have natural anti-inflammatory and antioxidant properties. It can help improve circulation, which might assist chickens in staying warm. Additionally, some poultry keepers believe that cinnamon can act as a respiratory health booster and possibly deter pests. Incorporating oatmeal and cinnamon as supplemental treats during winter can therefore offer both nutritional and health benefits for chickens.

WARNING: Never serve HOT oatmeal or soupy oatmeal on cold day.

As you turn the pages and discover these recipes, keep in mind the joy of eating in tune with the seasons. It's just another aspect of the harmonious co-existence we can foster with our chickens in our own backyards.

But remember, your chickens will still require their usual feed, these recipes are meant to be a fun and nutritious supplement, providing varied benefits as well as a change of routine for your chickens.

Chapter 3 Recipes By Month

January

Mo	Tu	We	Th	Fr	Sa	Su
1	2	3	4	5	6	7
8	9	10	11	12	13	14
15	16	17	18	19	20	21
22	23					
29	30					

February

Mo	Tu	We	Th	Fr	Sa	Su
			1	2	3	4
5	6	7	8	9	10	11
12	13	14	15	16	17	18
26	27	28	29	30	31	

March

Mo	Tu	We	Th	Fr	Sa	Su
				1	2	3
4	5	6	7	8	9	10
11	12	13	14	15	16	17
					23	24
					30	31

Feeding your animals according to the month and season is not only a fun and engaging activity, but it also provides numerous benefits for both you and your chickens. It supports their health and happiness while strengthening your bond with them! It's a rewarding experience that teaches you about responsibility, the cycles of nature, and the joy of caring for other creatures.

October

Mo	Tu	We	Th	Fr	Sa	Su
	1	2	3	4	5	6
7	8	9	10	11	12	13
14	15	16	17	18	19	20
21	22	23	24	25	26	27
28	29	30	31			

November

Mo	Tu	We	Th	Fr	Sa	Su
				1	2	3
4	5	6	7	8	9	10
11	12	13	14	15	16	17
18	19	20	21	22	23	24
25	26	27	28	29	30	

December

Mo	Tu	We	Th	Fr	Sa	Su
						1
2	3	4	5	6	7	8
9	10	11	12	13	14	15
16	17	18	19	20	21	22
23	24	25	26	27	28	29
30	31					

13. January

"IT'S BEEN A LONG WINTER"
PROTEIN PLATTER!

Ingredients
2 Cup Oats
1 Cup Sunflower Seeds
1 Cup Peas (Cooked)
2 Cups Greek Yogurt
4 Eggs (Cooked)
1 Can of tuna in water (no sodium)
2 Tablespoons Cayenne Pepper
Optional: Add cherry tomatoes and oregano to garnish!

15 MIN
15

Directions
1. Hard boil the eggs and chop them into pieces. Keep the eggshells and set them aside.
2. Bake the eggshells at 300 for 10 minutes, then grind them into a powder.
3. In a bowl, combine the oats, sunflower seeds, chopped eggs, and cayenne pepper.
4. In another bowl add the powdered eggshells to the tuna and mix well.
5. In the last bowl, mix together the greek yogurt and diced garlic.
6. Arrange the peas, and the mixtures onto a platter and enjoy!

14. February

NO-BAKE, PINK, OAT-BITES

Ingredients

1 Cup Old Fashioned Oats
1/2 Cup Ground Flax Seed
1/2 Cup Raisins
1 Tablespoon Chia Seed
1/3 Cup Honey
1/2 Cup Peanut Butter
(Optional) 1 tbsp of beet powder to make them pink!

1.5 HR

10

Directions

1. In a large bowl, combine the old fashioned oats, ground flax seed, raisins, chia seed, honey, and peanut butter.
2. Mix all the ingredients together until well combined.
3. Chill the dough in the fridge for 45 min. to 1hr.
4. After chilling, roll the dough into balls or use a cookie cutter to make fun shapes.

15. March

COOL AS A CUCUMBER SALAD

Ingredients

2-3 Large Cucumbers (Chopped)
1 Large Tomato (Chopped)
1/2 Cup Dill (Chopped)

Directions

1. Chop Cucumber, Tomato, and dill and combine together in a bowl.

 5 MIN

 5

Benefits

Cucumbers are a super healthy treat for your flock. They're full of antioxidants and are 96% water so they're great for keeping your chickens hydrated! Tomatoes are rich in antioxidants, fiber, and potassium as well as vitamins C, K, and B9, and are one of the most nutritious snacks for your chickens. Dill is a super herb that assists with the respiratory health and is also a very powerful antioxidant.

TIP: Make sure to always wash produce before feeding it to your flock. Most industrial farms treat their crops with poisonous pesticides and harmful fertilizers.

16. April

EASTER EGG CRUNCH

Ingredients

Shells from 1 dozen eggs
1 Tablespoon Cinnamon
1 Teaspoon Nutmeg
1 Tablespoon Hot Pepper Flakes
Cookie or sheet pan

Directions

1. Start by preheating your oven to 350 Degrees.
2. Place the egg shells on the sheet pan and bake for 25 min.
3. Once baked and cooled, crush the egg shells into small pieces.
4. Add the cinnamon, nutmeg, and hot pepper flakes to the shells.
5. Mix everything well and your ready to serve.

 25 MIN

 15+

TIP: If using leftover Easter Egg shells, Here are some chicken-safe natural dyes!
Red/Pink—Beets, raspberries, and cherries;
Yellow/Orange—Turmeric;
Green: Spirulina;
Blue/Purple: Acai, Red cabbage, and blueberries!

17. May

I HAVE ANOTHER MUFFIN?

Ingredients
1/2 Head of Cauliflower
1 Broccoli Stalk
6 Eggs
1/2 Cup Parsley

Directions
1. Preheat the oven to 350 and prepare a muffin pan.
2. Chop up the parsley, cauliflower & broccoli in a food processor.
3. Combine eggs and vegetable mix and stir until well mixed.
4. Pour mixture into a muffin pan (liners optional)
5. Bake for 20 minutes.
6. Let the muffins cool completely before feeding.

25 MIN

 10

Benefits
Cauliflower contains essential nutrients such as folic acid, vitamin B6, potassium, iron, phosphorous, magnesium, and more! Broccoli is beneficial as it provides vitamin K, vitamin C, potassium, zinc, calcium, and magnesium.

18. June

SUMMER SQUASH CASSEROLE

Ingredients

2 Yellow Squash
2 Zucchini Squash
6 Eggs
2 Tablespoons Oregano (Fresh)
3 Garlic Cloves (Minced)

Directions

1. Preheat your oven to 350°F
2. Slice the yellow and zucchini squash into 1/2-inch slices, keep the skin on.
3. Layer the slices in a casserole dish.
4. In a large mixing bowl, beat the eggs.
5. Add the fresh oregano and minced garlic to the beaten eggs.
6. Pour the egg mixture over the squash in the casserole dish, ensuring it's well-mixed.
7. Bake the casserole in the preheated oven for 40 minutes.
8. Allow the casserole to cool completely before serving.

 50 MIN

 10

19. July

FREEDOM FRUIT KABOBS

Ingredients

1 box of raspberries
1 box of blueberries
4 Apples
blunt stick skewers
Optional: Twine to tie around the skewer and to the ceiling of the run for an added element of enrichment.

5 MIN
15+

Directions

1. Core and cube apples.
2. Assemble fruit in red, white, and blue order.
3. Hangout with your chickens and share snacks!

20. August

WATERMELON SPLASH!

Ingredients

1 watermelon
Mint leaves
Pitted cherries

Directions

1. Cut the Watermelon in half.
2. Create "melon balls" with an ice cream scoop until all of the Watermelon is gone.
3. Refill the watermelon rind with chopped cherries, mint, and watermelon balls.
4. Serve and watch your chickens enjoy!

 5 MIN

 15+

Tip:

Cherries are a great source of vitamins like potassium, calcium, and vitamin C, and while the pits are edible they can be a choking hazard so it's best to avoid feeding them.

21. September

AUTUMN APPLES

Ingredients

1 Apple (Insides scooped out)
2 Tablespoons of Peanut butter
1 Tblsn of Black Sunflower seeds
1 Tablespoon mealworms
1 tsp Cinnamon

 10 MIN

 5

Directions

1. Take the core out of the apple to make room for the other ingredients
2. Mix in mealworms and sunflower seeds to unsalted peanut butter.
3. Stuff the apple with the mix and sprinkle cinnamon on top.

22. October

"TRICK OR TREATS"

Ingredients

One small pumpkin
1 Cup Oats
1 Cup Whole Wheat Flour
1/2 Cup Raisins
1/4 Cup Coconut Oil
2 Tablespoons Molasses
2 Teaspoons Allspice
(optional) mealworms for the trick!

 20 MIN

 10

Directions

1. Preheat your oven to 350°F (175°C).
2. In a large bowl, combine all of the dry ingredients: oats, whole wheat flour, raisins, and allspice.
3. hollow out and puree the pumpkin.
4. In a separate bowl, combine the hollowed and pureed pumpkin, coconut oil, and molasses.
5. Gradually add the wet ingredients to the dry ingredients. Fold them in well until all the dry ingredients are mixed together.
6. *If the mixture is too wet, add more oats until you reach the desired consistency.
7. Form the mixture into balls.
8. Place the balls on a baking sheet and bake for 15 minutes.
9. Allow the cookies to fully cool before serving. (opt.) add mealworms on top for the flock!

23. November

SHELL-ON ACORN SQUASH "PIE"

Ingredients

1 Acorn Squash
Cinnamon (to taste)
1 Cup Oats
1 Cup Feed
1/2 Cup dried berries
1/2 Cup sunflower seeds
1 Whole Garlic bulb (minced)
1/4 Cup coconut oil
1 Tablespoon molasses
1 Tablespoon Oregano or any other herbs your chickens like

 40 MIN

10

Directions

1. Preheat your oven to 350°F (175°C).
2. Cut the squash in half and place it flesh side down on a baking tray.
3. Bake for about 30 minutes.
4. Once the squash has cooled, remove the flesh and seeds and place them in a bowl.
5. Mash the insides with a fork.
6. In the same bowl, add oats, feed, dried berries, sunflower seeds, minced garlic, coconut oil, molasses, and your chosen herbs.
6. Mix all of the ingredients together really well.
7. Once the mixture is well combined, place it back into the skins.

24. December

CHRISTMAS COOKIES FOR SANTA CAWS

Ingredients

1/2 Cup Coconut Oil
1/4 Cup Honey
2 Eggs
1/2 Cup Whole Wheat Flour
1/2 Cup Wheat Germ
1/2 Cup Cornmeal
1 Teaspoon Baking soda
1 Teaspoon Cinnamon
1 Cup Raisins

 20 MIN

 10

Directions

1. Pre-heat oven to 350 degrees
2. Beat oil and honey until creamy.
3. Add the 2 eggs.
4. Combine flour, wheat germ, cornmeal, raisins, baking soda, and cinnamon with the oil and honey mixture and blend until creamy.
5. Drop dough onto an ungreased cookie sheet using an ice cream scoop.
6. Bake for 10 minutes.
7. Allow to cool completely before serving

| 4.1 "Essential" and "Additional" Diet Components | 4.2 Vitamin Deficiencies | 4.3 Common Issues & Dietary Support | 4.4 Chicken 9-1-1 |

CHAPTER 4 CHICKEN REARING CHALLENGES & DIETARY SUPPORT

In this chapter, we'll delve into a variety of recipes that offer holistic health benefits to your chickens, by focusing on ingredients renowned for their wellness aids and benefits. The following recipes focus on a wide range of specific issues that you may encounter on your journey as a chicken tender! However, it is important to keep in mind that while certain foods can address specific issues, a balanced diet is crucial. And while these ingredient-let recipes will certainly help, they will never take the place of a poultry veterinarian or an experienced chicken keeper for advice specific to your flock's needs or concerns.

4.1 "Essential" and "Additional" Diet Components

Essentials:

Proteins: are crucial for growth and repair in chickens. Contrary to some beliefs, chickens are not vegetarians. Protein-rich foods include insects, meat, and even eggs occasionally. They are an important factor in feather growth and egg-laying.

Vegetables or "Greens": are packed with vitamins and nutrients. They also provide the necessary fiber for optimal digestion, and nutrient absorption. Which is why, greens eaten from free ranging time are incredibly important.

Grains: Grains are an excellent source of energy due to their carbohydrate content. Certain grains also supply essential amino acids, which are the building blocks of proteins.

Nuts, Legumes, and/or Seeds: These are sources of healthy fats and provide sustained energy. They are also a good source of protein and fiber.

Additionals:

Fruits: Fruits are a source of immediate energy due to their natural sugars. They also contain antioxidants that contribute to overall health and may even help prevent diseases. The high water content aids in hydration.

Herbs: are rich in various antioxidants and many possess anti-inflammatory properties. The benefits of herbs are so diverse and specific to the plants; some support vascular health, others can mitigate stress, and a select few can even act as natural pest repellents. ***

Flowers: Certain edible flowers can offer a range of nutrients, including vitamins and minerals. They can add diversity to a chicken's diet and may have various health benefits depending on the type of flower.

*** *Specific benefits are listed in the back of the book, per ingredient, in alphabetical order, and also by category of ingredient.*

4.2 Vitamin Deficiencies

Vitamin deficiencies in chickens can manifest in various ways, and this is not an exhaustive list, but depending on the specific vitamin that is lacking there are physical and behavioral clues. Here are some signs to look out for:

Vitamin : Deficiency Symptoms

A: Poor growth, decreased egg production, weakness, and a decrease in resistance to diseases. Their eyes may also show signs such as conjunctivitis, discharge, or even blindness in severe cases.

D: This is often associated with rickets in young birds, characterized by weak, soft, or deformed bones. In laying hens, it can lead to soft-shelled eggs and decreased egg production. Vitamin D is affected by the amount of sunlight the birds get.

E: This can lead to muscular dystrophy, and decreased hatchability of eggs.

B: A deficiency in B vitamins can result in a multitude of health issues in chickens, such as stunted growth, general weakness, and neurological problems. These neurological issues can manifest as ataxia, which is a lack of muscle control, involuntary twitching, circular walking patterns, and even convulsions. Thiamine, a crucial B vitamin, can be inhibited by certain medicated feeds. For instance, feeds medicated with Amprolium, a common treatment for coccidiosis, can potentially interfere with thiamine absorption due to its mechanism of action. Therefore, it's important to manage the use of such feeds carefully to prevent thiamine deficiency.

K: This can lead to prolonged blood clotting times, leading to excessive bleeding even from minor wounds.

C: Vitamin C, also known as ascorbic acid, is a nutrient that most birds, including chickens, can synthesize on their own. This makes vitamin C deficiency in chickens quite rare. However, under certain circumstances, such as extreme stress or poor diet, chickens might not produce enough vitamin C and show signs like a general weakness or susceptibility to disease, anemia, and deteriorating feather quality.

Remember, these are just potential signs and may also be indicative of other health issues. If you suspect a vitamin deficiency, it's important to consult with a poultry veterinarian for a proper diagnosis and treatment plan.

4.3 COMMON ISSUES & DIETARY SUPPORT

Maintaining a healthy flock requires an understanding of common health issues and the effective strategies that address them. A balanced diet, guided by a holistic approach, and complemented by timely responses, can significantly enhance the well-being of your chickens. This section will delve into common health problems and their dietary supports by exploring various food types. Embracing the philosophy of "let food be thy medicine and medicine be thy food," we will discuss typical challenges faced by chicken owners and the recipes that can help manage them.

25. Omega-3 Power Snacks

 FLOCK OF 5    2HRS

Ingredients
1/2 cup Flaxseeds.

1 cup unsalted nut butter

Instructions:
1. Grind the flaxseeds in a coffee grinder or food processor to make a fine powder.
2. In a bowl, mix the ground flaxseeds with unsalted nut butter to form a thick paste.
3. Roll the mixture into small balls or shape them into bite-sized treats.
4. Place the omega-3 power snacks in the refrigerator for a few hours to set.
5. Serve the snacks to your chickens as a protein-rich treat.

DECREASED EGG PRODUCTION
Chickens naturally go through cycles of high and low egg production.
In the fall and winter months, when the days are short and cold, and the likelihood of their offspring's survival also decreases, so does egg production. This time period is also necessary for the bird to recoup a lot of its nutrition lost during high production periods. However, during normal periods of laying, a decrease in egg production can often be addressed through dietary adjustments, pending that the birds feel safe enough in their environment to lay. The first step would be increasing the protein and fatty acids, or Omega-3s, in their diet.

26. Fancy-Feather Fish Tacos

 FLOCK OF 15+  15 MIN

Ingredients:
1 cup of sunflower seeds
1 can of tuna fish (in water)
2 hard-boiled eggs (chopped)
2 cups of finely chopped kale
1/2 of black solider fly larva
(I.e. GrubTerra)
2-3 hardshell corn tacos
3 tbsp of water

Instructions:
1. In a large bowl, combine the sunflower seeds, & tuna fish (undrained).
2. Add mix as base of the tacos.
3. Add the Kale on top.
4. Mash the hard-boiled eggs & add the water to make an egg-salsa. Add to the top of the tacos.
5. Serve the snack in a clean, shallow dish or in a taco stand.

FEATHER LOSS AND INFERIOR FEATHER QUALITY
Feather issues can be caused by non-dietary factors such as stress, mites, or pecking/over mating behavior, so it's important to consider the overall health and environment of your chickens. However diet is still a factor and while there isn't a one-size-fits-all dietary solution, certain nutrients can contribute to feather growth and overall health, potentially mitigating feather loss such as: Protein—specifically keratin, amino acids—such as methionine, vitamins and minerals—such as vitamin B12, biotin, zinc, and copper, and fats are also important for feather health.

27. Whole-Egg Veggie Bake

 FLOCK OF 15   1HR

Ingredients
1 Bag of fresh or frozen green beans
1 Bag of Kale
10 Whole Eggs with shells included!
1/2 Cup Flax seed
1 Tablespoon Oregano (Fresh)
1 Tablespoon Parsley (Fresh)

Instructions:
1. Preheat your oven to 350°F (175°C).
2. In a large bowl, whisk the eggs until well blended.
3. Add the green beans, flax seed, fresh oregano, and fresh parsley to the egg mixture.
4. Stir until everything is well combined.
5. Pour the mixture into a casserole dish.
6. Bake the casserole in the preheated oven for 45 minutes.

*it's not advisable to feed raw green beans to your chickens as they contain trace amounts of lectin. Always ensure any green beans are cooked.

CALCIUM DEFICIENCY / SOFT EGGSHELLS

A common and effective method to address calcium deficiency in chickens, which often results in soft eggshells, is to add oyster shell to their feed. Oyster shell is rich in calcium and its rough texture allows it to remain in the chicken's digestive system for an extended period, providing a steady supply of calcium. Crushed eggshells, once cleaned and dried, can also be given back to the chickens, effectively recycling the calcium. However, it's important to crush them thoroughly to prevent promoting egg-eating habits among the flock. Dark leafy vegetables such as kale are also good choices. They not only supply calcium but also boost overall health with their high vitamin content. Lastly, it's crucial to remember that vitamin D plays a key role in calcium absorption. Making sure your chickens get enough sunlight or supplementing their diet with vitamin D can improve the effectiveness of these dietary interventions. It doesn't do any good to supply the nutrient if the body cant absorb it due to some other deficiency, echoing yet again the importance of a balanced diet.

28. Crustless Spice Pie

 FLOCK OF 15+   2HRS

INGREDIENTS
1 Baking Pumpkin
1/2 Cup Wheat Bran
2 Eggs
1 Tablespoon Cinnamon
1/2 Teaspoon Ground Ginger
1/4 Teaspoon Ground Cloves
1 Tablespoon Probiotics
Pie Pan (No crust)

INSTRUCTIONS:
1. Preheat oven to 400
2. Bake pumpkin for 45 minutes until the flesh is soft
3. Scoop out the flesh and seeds if there are any and place in a large mixing bowl
4. In a large bowl beat the eggs and pumpkin together.
5. Add in the cinnamon, ginger and cloves
6. Pour the mixture into the pan and bake for 40 to 50 minutes
7. Cool completely then sprinkle probiotics on the top

Notes: Ginger aids in relaxing and soothing the intestinal tract and inhibits the formation of inflammatory compounds, and Cloves enhance the intestinal microbiota population

DIGESTIVE ISSUES AND/OR DIARRHEA
Incorporate probiotics which are found in fermented foods like yogurt, to enhance gut health and nutrient absorption. Feeding fermented feed periodically is an excellent way to enhance gut health and boost the immune system. Fiber-rich foods such as oats and barley can help solidify loose stools. Apple cider vinegar in drinking water can balance crop and gut pH, discouraging harmful bacteria and fungus. Pumpkin, which is high in fiber and contains the anti-parasite cucurbitacin, is beneficial in some cases as well. Herbs like oregano and thyme, known for their antimicrobial and antiparasitic properties respectively, can also help.

29. Go Bananas, Bites

 FLOCK OF 5    1.5HRS

INGREDIENTS
2 over-ripe bananas, mashed.
1 cup of cooked peas, mashed
2 cups of cooked corn, mashed
1 cup of kale, minced
1 tablespoon of fish oil
1 cup of shelled, unsalted, sunflower seeds.

INSTRUCTIONS:
1. In a large mixing bowl, combine the bananas, peas, and corn.
2. Mix until well incorporated
3. Mix in the chopped leafy greens.
4. Drizzle the mixture with fish oil. Refrigerate for one hour.
5. Scoop out desired bite-sizes and roll into a ball.
6. Roll the balls out into the seeds
7. Serve immediately to your chickens, ensuring each bird gets a bite!

MOLTING PERIODS AND/OR ENERGY DEPLETION

During molting periods and instances of energy depletion, chickens can greatly benefit from a diet rich in protein and certain vitamins. High-protein foods like mealworms, sunflower seeds, and peas can help in feather regrowth during molting, as feathers are approximately 85% protein. For energy replenishment, grains such as corn and oats are excellent, providing complex carbohydrates for sustained energy release. Additionally bananas can provide quick energy due to their natural sugars. Vitamin-rich leafy greens, such as kale, can support overall health and vitality. Kale is rich in vitamins K, A, and C, supporting skin health, feather health, and immune function, respectively. Lastly, adding a bit of fish oil to their feed can provide essential fatty acids.

30. Calming Spray

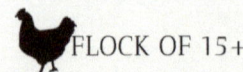 FLOCK OF 15+    15 MIN

Ingredients:
1 cup chopped lemon balm
1 cup lavender leaves / flowers
1 cup vodka

Instructions:
1. In a one-quart mason jar, combine the lemon balm, lavender leaves and flowers, and vodka.
2. Allow the mixture to sit and macerate for 2 to 4 weeks.
3. After the maceration period, strain the herbs out and transfer the liquid to a new glass jar.
4. To use, pour the tincture at full strength into a glass spray bottle.
5. Spray the tincture onto surfaces in your coop and nest boxes.

STRESS AND ANXIETY

Chickens, like many animals, can experience stress and anxiety, which can manifest in altered behavior, reduced egg production, and overall health decline. Various factors, from environmental changes to predators, can trigger these responses, underscoring the importance of a stable and safe environment for poultry.

31. Breath-Easy Fried Rice

🐔 FLOCK OF 15+   🕐 30MIN

INGREDIENTS

2 Cups of cooked wild grain rice
2 Eggs
2 Garlic Cloves
1 Cup Frozen Mixed vegetables
1/2 Cup Coconut Oil
1 tbsp Cinnamon
1 tbsp or 3 stems of leaves of Thyme
1 tsp or 4-5 stems of Oregano

INSTRUCTIONS

1. Heat up a skillet or large pan.
2. Scramble the eggs in the pan.
3. Add the cooked wild grain rice to the pan. Allow it to cook for about 5 minutes, tossing it with the scrambled eggs and coconut oil for moisture.
4. Add the garlic and frozen mixed vegetables to the pan. Combine all the ingredients well.
5. Cook everything together for about 15 min.
6. Mix in Cinnamon, Thyme, and Oregano.
7. Allow the fried rice to cool before serving.

TIP: Rice is a good source of essential nutrients such as magnesium, selenium, thiamine, niacin, and pyridoxine, which are crucial in combating vitamin deficiency that can lead to compromised immune systems.

RESPIRATORY ISSUES

Respiratory issues in chickens can manifest as sneezing, coughing, wheezing, or discharge from the nose or eyes. A diet rich in Vitamin A can support respiratory health, and foods such as carrots, peas, and leafy greens are excellent sources of this vitamin. Additionally, certain herbs like cinnamon, garlic, thyme, and oregano have antimicrobial properties that can further bolster respiratory health. However, it's important to note that respiratory issues in chickens can be serious and often require veterinary attention. They can be caused by various factors, including infectious diseases, poor air quality, or environmental stressors.

Luna

WWW.SANITYRANCH.CO

Twinky

Mr. Rip

32. Broccoli Sprouts Quiche (DF)

 FLOCK OF 5    2HRS

INGREDIENTS
4 whole eggs.
2 Cups of Broccoli sprouts
-1/2 Cup Flax Seed
4 Garlic Cloves (Minced)
1 Tablespoon Probiotics (Probios sprinkle on top after the dish has fully cooled the heat will kill the live bacteria in the probiotics)
1 Tablespoon Hot Pepper Flakes

Instructions:
1. Preheat your oven to 400°F (200°C).
2. Boil the broccoli in water until it's defrosted if using frozen, or until it's soft if using fresh.
3. In a large bowl, mix together the eggs, flax seed, and minced garlic cloves.
4. Place the cooked broccoli in a casserole pan.
5. Pour the egg mixture over the broccoli in the pan, and mix well to combine.
6. Bake the casserole in the preheated oven for 45 minutes.
7. Allow the casserole to cool before serving.

VITAMIN DEFICIENCIES/OR LOW SUNLIGHT EXPOSURE
In chickens, sunlight exposure promotes the synthesis of vitamin D, essential for calcium metabolism and bone health, and while they can produce their own vitamin C, it plays a crucial role in combating oxidative stress and supporting overall health..Vitamin deficiencies in chickens can lead to a range of health issues and are often identifiable through specific signs. Vitamin D deficiency is one of the most common deficiencies in chickens. To prevent and treat Vitamin D deficiency, ensure that chickens have access to sunlight, and are fed a well-balanced feed.
See Chapter 4.2 For More Details.

Wholesome Ingredients

Fresh, locally sourced ingredients are the secret to a healthy meal.

33. ACV TINCTURE

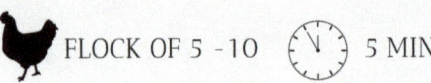 FLOCK OF 5 -10   5 MIN

INGREDIENTS
1 Gallon Water
1 Tablespoon ACV (Must be the brand with "The Mother")
1/4 Teaspoon Acidified Copper Sulfate

INSTRUCTIONS:
1. Mix the ACV and ACS in a gallon of water and stir well.
2. Treat for 7-10 days until the sour crop has cleared up.
3. Make sure to provide fresh clean water everyday during this treatment.

SOUR CROP
Sour crop is a common digestive disorder in chickens, characterized by a delay in the emptying of the crop, which is a pouch in a chicken's neck where food is stored and softened before continuing on to the stomach. This delay can lead to fermentation and the growth of yeast, causing the crop to become swollen and squishy. Chickens with sour crop may exhibit signs such as a bad (or sour) smell from the beak, loss of appetite, lethargy, and regurgitation of foul-smelling fluid. Causes can include ingestion of long grass, fibrous or tough foods, or foreign objects that block the crop, as well as bacterial or fungal infections. ACV can be therapeutic in some cases but it is important to contact your local avian vet if you suspect sour crop. Treatment often involves emptying the crop, by withholding food or otherwise, followed by administration of antifungal compounds and probiotics to restore healthy gut flora.

34. Swinging Head O' Cabbage

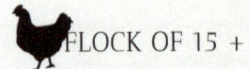 FLOCK OF 15 +  5 MIN

INGREDIENTS
1 head of Cabbage
1 sting or Twine

INSTRUCTIONS:
Hang the cabbage from the ceiling of the run for the flock to peck at and alleviate any boredom.

INSUFFICIENT FORAGING OPPORTUNITIES

Scatter or hang leafy greens, herbs, or vegetable scraps in the coop or run to simulate natural foraging activity and stimulate their minds. You can also hide treats like mealworms or sunflower seeds in between the leaves.

35. Immune-Boosting Broth

 FLOCK OF 10    1.5 HRS

Ingredients:
3 cups of vegetable broth (Low Sodium)
Water
Fresh herbs (oregano, thyme, rosemary, echinacea, & parsley)
1/2 garlic clove
1 teaspoon apple cider vinegar (optional)

Instructions:
Add fresh herbs and garlic cloves to the pot of broth.
Bring the mixture to a boil, then reduce the heat and let it
simmer for an hour. Allow the broth to cool. Optional: Add apple cider vinegar. Serve the immune-boosting broth to your chickens in their water or as a stand alone warm treat. **Warning: DO NOT SERVE HOT.**

IMMUNE SYSTEM WEAKNESS

Chickens with weak immune systems are more susceptible to a range of health issues. By incorporating certain herbs into their diet periodically they can regain some strength and vitality. In this broth: Thyme supports respiratory health with its antimicrobial properties. Rosemary provides antioxidant and anti-inflammatory benefits. Parsley, rich in vitamins and minerals like vitamin C and iron, contributes to overall health. Echinacea is known for its immunity-boosting properties, but feel free to use the index at the end of the book to customize your broth to your specific needs.

36. Meatloaf for Irritated Chickens

 FLOCK OF 15+    1.5HRS

Ingredients:
3 Eggs (Beaten)
3/4 Cup Milk
2 Tablespoon Molasses
2/3 Cup Old Fashioned Oats
2/3 Cup of Chicken Feed
1/4 Cup Wheat Germ
4 Garlic Cloves (Minced)
2 Tbsn Dried Oregano
1.5 lbs of Ground Beef
1 can of pumpkin
(Optional) top loaf with Nasturtium flower petals.

Instructions
1. Preheat your oven to 350°F (175°C).
2. In a large bowl, combine the beaten eggs, milk, pumpkin, and molasses.
3. Stir in the old-fashioned oats, chicken feed, wheat germ, minced garlic, and dried oregano.
4. Add the ground beef to the mixture and mix well until all ingredients are well combined.
5. Transfer the mixture into a casserole pan.
6. Bake the meatloaf in the preheated oven for 1 hour.
7. Allow the meatloaf to cool completely before serving to your chickens.

PARASITES

Chickens can fall prey to both external parasites (mites, lice) and internal ones (worms). These parasites can decrease egg production and cause discomfort. Garlic, when regularly added to their feed, is believed by many to act as a natural deterrent. Food-grade diatomaceous earth, used for dusting the coop and chickens, can kill mites and lice but can cause respiratory problems if used while occupied or the coop isn't well ventilated, First Saturday Lime is an alternative that is less of an irritant but is still effective. Many seasoned chicken keepers add oregano and sometimes crushed pumpkin seeds to their feed or water to act as a natural preventative. Moreover, Nasturtium supports respiratory health and can act as a natural antiparasitic.

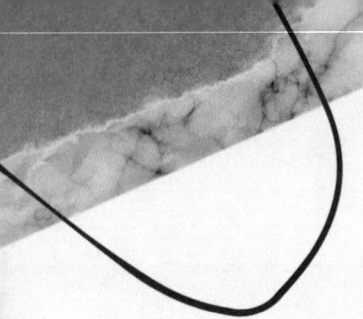

37. Boredom Buster Block (2.8 Lbs)

 FLOCK OF 15+  2HRS

INGREDIENTS
2 Cups Scratch
1 Cup Pellets
1 Cup Whole Oats
1/2 Cup Black Sunflower seeds
1/2 Cup Molasses
1/2 Cup Coconut Oil
1/4 Cup Wheat Germ
1/4 Cup Whole Wheat Flour
3 Eggs
1 Tsp Cayenne Pepper
1 Tsp Cinnamon

INSTRUCTIONS:
Preheat oven to 325 degrees
Mix the dry ingredients together until blended.
Mix the wet ingredients into the dry
Place the mixture into a loaf pan and cook for 30 minutes.
If you want to hang the block go ahead and put a hole where you want the rope to go.
Once the block has completely cooled it will harden up and you can feed it.
(optional) Garnish with Lemon Balm which is known to have a calming and anti-aggression effect on chickens.

AGGRESSION AND/OR BOREDOM

Bored chickens can resort to pecking at each other. Giving them enough space to roam and adding enrichment like perches, mirrors, or hanging treats can prevent this. Happiness is a factor in health and enrichment matters! This is the ultimate enrichment treat for your flock. Let them take out their aggression on the block and not each other while reaping the benefits of a powerhouse list of ingredients; Oats, whether raw or cooked, offer a nutritious snack packed with essential minerals and vitamins. Black sunflower seeds, rich in vitamin E, promote healthy skin, feathers, egg production, and fertility, while also providing calcium. Molasses is a good source of calcium, iron, potassium, and magnesium. Coconut oil, known for its potential heart health benefits, contains caprylic and lauric acid, which can strengthen the immune system. Wheat germ, rich in vitamin E, supports healthy skin and feather growth, making it essential during molting and breeding seasons. Whole wheat flour aids digestion and can enhance your flock's resistance to coccidiosis. Cayenne pepper stimulates the circulatory and digestive systems, boosting egg production. Lastly, cinnamon, with its anti-microbial, anti-inflammatory, and antioxidant properties, can help prevent respiratory infections in your flock.

Silkie Acres

**You can also purchase pre-made boredom blocks directly from Silkie Acres

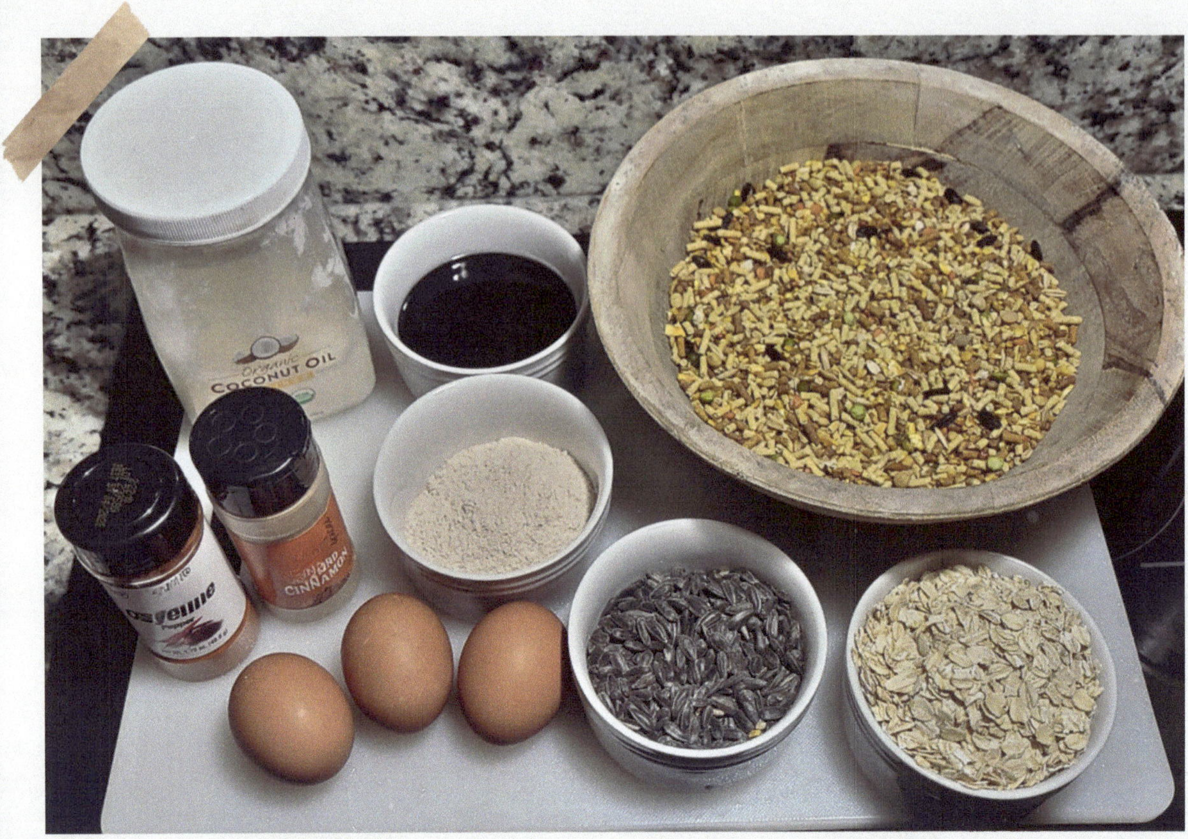
Organic
COCONUT OIL
CINNAMON

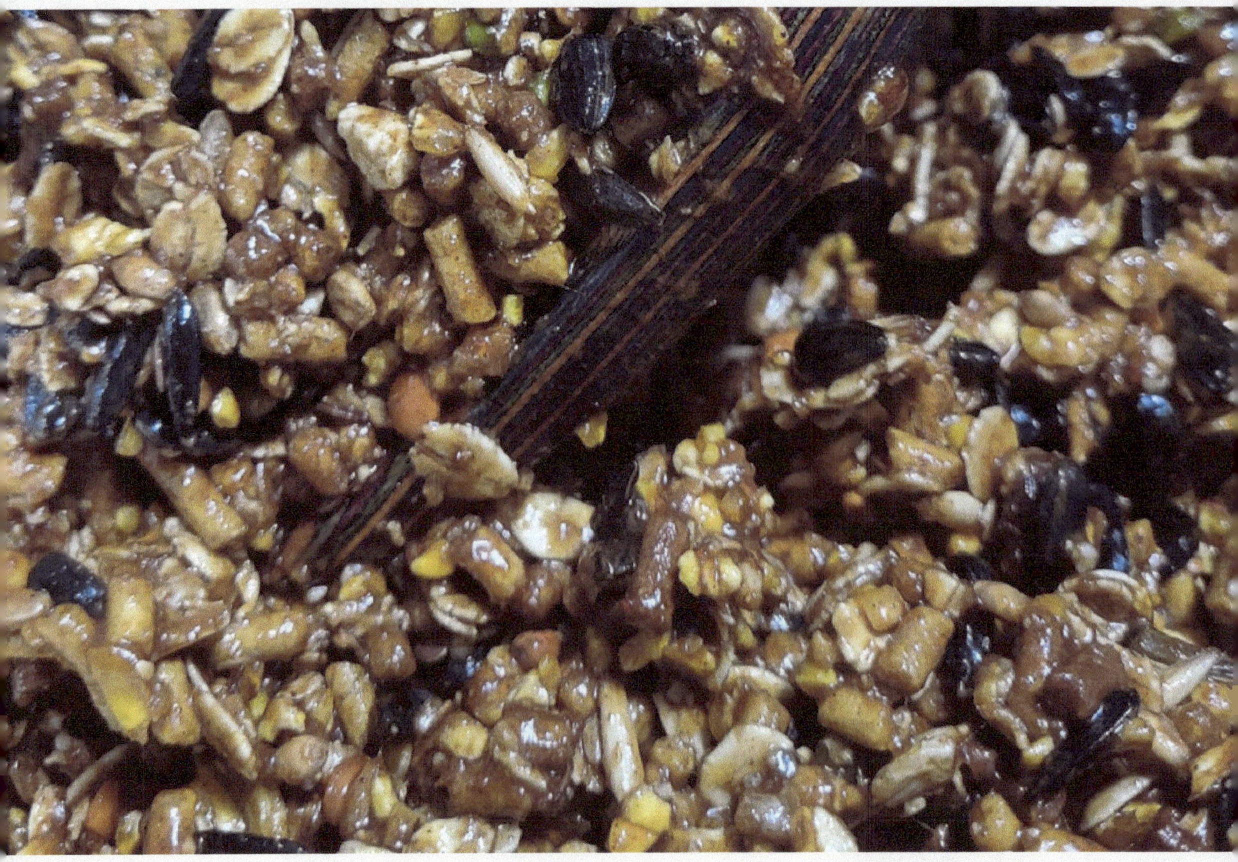

Extreme Cold

In extreme cold, ensure your chicken coop is well-insulated but also ventilated in areas that will not get a lot of drafts. Both must be achieved to balance warmth and moisture control. Use warm bedding materials like hemp or wood shavings, and provide fresh, unfrozen water regularly— Preferably use waterers with nipples to avoid splashes or dips. Increase feed quantity as chickens burn more calories to stay warm. Monitor your flock for signs of frostbite on their combs, wattles, and toes.

See Chapter 2.1 on Winter Recipes

Heat Stress

During hot months, provide shaded areas in the coop and ample fresh water. Adding electrolytes to their water can help maintain hydration, and Remember chickens will be reluctant to drink water hotter than their body heat (about 100 degrees.) Consider offering cool treats like frozen fruits or vegetables. Maintain a dust bath area for self-cooling, and/or provide cool bricks to stand on. Monitor your chickens for signs of heat stress; panting is your first sign that they are too hot. Lethargy and decreased egg production will also occur. Take cooling measures if these signs appear (ice. fans, kiddie pools).

See Chapter 2.1 on Summer Recipes.

Bear in mind that chickens are unique, and what works for one may not work for all. Regularly observe your chickens and adjust their care accordingly. By incorporating these healthy boosts into your chickens' diet, you can enhance their immune system, promote vitality, and support their overall health. Experiment with different ingredients and observe the benefits they bring to your feathered friends. Remember to introduce new foods gradually and ensure they are appropriate for your specific flock's dietary needs. It's important to note that while certain foods can help alleviate certain issues, they should be provided in moderation and as part of a balanced diet. Consult with a poultry veterinarian or an expert chicken keeper for specific recommendations tailored to your flock's needs.

4.4 Chicken 9-1-1

Rearing backyard chickens is a gratifying experience, but it does come with challenges. Chickens can suffer from various diseases, but some are more often encountered than others, and unfortunately in most of the cases listed below, prevention is your best case of action. In fact, most will need quick action, isolation, and veterinary care. Here is a common list of diseases that will need to be immediately managed by a veterinarian and not something you can attempt to rectify via diet.

Diseases:

1. **Coccidiosis:** This parasitic disease affects the intestinal tract of chickens. Prevention can be achieved by supplementing the chickens' diet with coccidiostats. Consider incorporating wheat germ into their feed for added nutrition. Medicated feed can also be beneficial in managing this condition.

2. **Avian Influenza (Bird Flu):** This viral disease doesn't have a dietary remedy. However, a balanced and nutritious diet can help strengthen the chickens' immune system and promote overall health, aiding in disease resistance. *If you suspect your chickens have this, please report it immediately to the appropriate authorities. In the U.S. you can call the* USDA at 1-866-536-7593.

3. **Marek's Disease:** This viral disease leads to tumor formation in chickens. While there's no dietary cure, maintaining a balanced diet can support overall health and immunity, helping the chickens to better cope with the disease.

4. **Fowl Cholera**: This bacterial infection can be severe in backyard flocks. Antibiotics are the primary treatment, but adding probiotics to the diet can support gut health and potentially help prevent bacterial diseases.

5. **Infectious Bronchitis**: This respiratory disease is caused by a virus. There's no dietary remedy, but a balanced diet can support overall health and resilience, helping chickens to better withstand the disease.

40. First Response ER Tonic

INGREDIENTS

1 egg yolk (no white)
1 gallon of spring water
1 packet of Save-a-Chick electrolytes
1 packet of Save-a-Chick probiotics
1 ml of Nutri-Drench
Optional: 1 ml of Apple Cider Vinegar (ACV), particularly if you suspect sour crop.

DIRECTIONS

1. Empty both Save a Chick packets into a 1 gallon jug of spring water.
2. Combine the 1/4 of a cup out of the gallon mixture, the yolk, the Nutridrench, and the ACV (if using) into a clean, and preferably sterile, container.
3. Mix them thoroughly until well combined.

**If your chicken is unable or unwilling to drink the solution, you can soak a Q-tip in the tonic and gently press it against the chicken's closed beak. The chicken's reflexes should prompt it to consume the liquid.

Warning: Avoid forcing liquid directly into a birds mouth. Chickens can easily inhale the liquid into their lungs, which can lead to infections or choking. Always prioritize the safety and comfort of your chicken when administering this tonic.

Chapter 5

Love Spells

This chapter is appropriately nicknamed love spells because with these treats your chickens will instantly fall in love with you (if they aren't already). Although may only last for the duration of the treats. These scrumptious creations will serve as special rewards and bring joy to your feathered friends, but it's important to remember, treats should make up no more than 5-10% of your chickens' diet. The rest of their diet should be balanced chicken feed that provides all the nutrients they need.

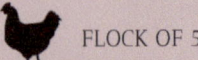 FLOCK OF 5   O/N

41. Mealworm Popsicles

Ingredients

1 cup mealworms (dried)
2 cups water
Fresh herbs (ie Mint)
2 cups unsweetened yogurt

TIP: Get a mini-blender for your chicken treats!

Method

1. Soak the worms in water for a few minutes to rehydrate.
2. Blend the mealworms, yogurt, and water.
3. Add a few fresh herbs for added flavor and nutrition.
4. Pour the mixture into ice cube trays or popsicle molds.
5. Place the trays or molds in the freezer.
6. Freeze overnight.
7. Remove the popsicles from the molds and serve to your chickens as a cool and protein-rich treat.

 FLOCK OF 10  15 MIN

42. Scrambled Egg Surprise

Ingredients

6 eggs 1/4 cup of water

1 can of mixed vegetables (carrots, peas, corn, etc.)

1/2 cup of oats

1/4 cup of unsalted peanuts (optional)

1/4 cup of mealworms

Warning: make sure that your chickens tolerate peanuts well before serving this treat or make it without the peanuts.

Method

1. Crack the eggs into a bowl, add the water, and whisk them until the yolks and whites are fully combined.
2. Heat a non-stick pan over medium heat. Once the pan is hot, add the whisked eggs.
3. Let the eggs cook without stirring for a few moments until they start to set around the edges. Then, gently stir the eggs with a spatula, pushing them from the edges toward the center.
4. Continue to cook, stirring occasionally, until the eggs are mostly cooked but still slightly runny.
5. Add the mixed vegetables, oats, and (crushed) peanuts to the pan.
6. Stir everything together until well combined.
7. Continue to cook the mixture, stirring occasionally, until the eggs are fully cooked and the vegetables are warmed through.
8. Remove the pan from the heat and let the scrambled egg mixture cool completely before serving it to your chickens.
9. .. Once cooled, top with mealworms and serve!

FLOCK OF 10   10 MIN

43. O-mega Tuna Party

Ingredients

2 cans of tuna in water.

1 cup of unflavored Greek yogurt.

1/4 cup of ground flax or chia seeds.

1 tsp of cayenne pepper

Method

1. Combine tuna, yogurt, and seeds. (do not drain tuna cans.)
2. Serve and enjoy!

TIP: Put in three different bowls so that the bottom of the pecking order have a chance to grab some too! This will go fast!

 FLOCK OF 10   25 MIN

44. Healthy Birthday Cake!

Ingredients

1/2 Cup Whole Wheat Flour
1/2 Cup Water
1/2 Cup Creamy Peanut Butter
1 Tsp Baking Soda
1 Apple Diced
6 Strawberries Chopped
Coconut Oil for greasing cake molds
Optional
1 Cup of whipped yogurt
1 Tbsp of Millet

Method

1. Preheat oven to 350 Degrees
2. Grease your cake molds
3. Combine flour, water, peanut butter, and baking powder in a bowl.
4. Mix until combined
5. Add the apples and strawberries
6. Pour batter into the mold of your choice
7. Bake for 20 mins
8. (Optional) Add whipped Greek yogurt as the icing and millet for the sprinkles!

By incorporating these homemade treats into your chickens' routine, you'll witness the joy and excitement they bring. Indulge your feathered friends with these delectable creations, and cherish the moments of happiness they inspire. Always remember to serve with fresh clean water!

| 6.1 Types of Sprouts | 6.2 Methods of Sprouting |

CHAPTER 6 SPROUTS

Sprouting seeds for your backyard chickens is a simple and cost-effective way to boost your flock's nutrition. They're packed with vitamins, minerals, and protein—and chickens absolutely love the texture and taste of them! Sprouts also provide a perfect opportunity for them to engage in their natural foraging and scratching behavior. This chapter will guide you through the process of growing sprouts, discuss different types of sprouts, introduce three methods of sprouting, and explain the benefits of sprouts for your chickens.

6.1 Types of Sprouts

There are many types of seeds that can be sprouted for chickens. Each offer unique nutritional benefits and increases the omega-3 levels in the eggs. Sprouts are also abundant in fiber, vitamin C, proteins, and calcium. They can be consumed daily and have been known to aid in heart health, immunity, vision, and digestion.

Alfalfa Sprouts: These are rich in vitamins and minerals. They're also a good source of protein.

Broccoli Sprouts: offer a lot of nutrition for our feathered friends. It offers vitamins A & C, iron, calcium, and fiber. All these combined improve the immune system, and red blood cell production, keep the bones strong, and aid in digestion. They also have a nice crunch that chickens love.

Lentil Sprouts: Lentil Sprouts are low in fat and an excellent source of protein, potassium, and antioxidants. Lentils also contain zinc, magnesium, iron, potassium, and B Vitamins.

Wheat Sprouts: Wheat sprouts are a good source of vitamins & minerals, and are also easy to grow. They're a personal favorite to grow and feed to our flocks and families. Wheat Grass can cover 15 - 20% of a chicken's whole diet. It's enriched with nutritional elements such as chlorophyll, amino acids, minerals, enzymes, vitamins, and energy.

Arugula Sprouts: reduce the risks of cancer, improves eyesight, strengthen the brain, and help the body absorb minerals. Arugula also boosts the immune system.

Flax Seed Sprouts: have been known to increase the omega-3 in eggs laid by hens that consume them. Flax is considered a superfood. If you want healthy chickens laying good quality eggs I suggest sprouting some flax seed for them. Flax seeds and sprouts will also produce healthier chicks from your hens as well.

Radish Sprouts: are rich in essential amino acids and chlorophyll which has all sorts of benefits from cancer-fighting properties to digestive aid. They also contain vitamins A, B, C, E, and K, calcium, iron, magnesium, phosphorus, potassium, and zinc.

Chia Seed Sprouts: have numerous benefits such as lowering blood pressure, improved blood sugar control, and high fiber and omega-3 levels. Chia sprouts are highly beneficial for the cardiovascular system by keeping the heart healthy and allowing nutrients and oxygen to flow properly.

SPROUTS

Silkie Acres

6.2 Methods of Sprouting

Sprouts are a powerhouse of nutrition for your chickens. They're high in vitamins, minerals, and protein, and they're also easier to digest than unsprouted seeds. This means your chickens can absorb more of the nutrients. Sprouts also provide a source of fresh greens, which can be particularly beneficial during the winter months, when grass and bugs are scarce, or whenever your flock isn't getting as much free range time as desired.

There are several methods for sprouting seeds, but we'll focus on the three simplest methods: the Jar Method, the Tray Method, and the Kiddie-Pool Method.

Jar Method:
Place a jar full of your preferred seeds in water on a window sill with direct sunlight. Soak them for about three hours and then rinse them daily until they sprout. It's a simple method that doesn't require much space, time, or equipment.

Tray Method:
This method involves spreading seeds out in a tray, keeping them moist, and allowing them to sprout. You will need either a plant light or a window that gets decent sunlight. Soak the grain or seeds for at least 3 hours to initiate the germination process. Place the drained seeds in the tray with the dome cover or a wet paper towel (use sprouting trays with drainage holes). Rinse the seeds twice a day to prevent molding. Small white sprouts will begin to appear by day 2, and by day 5-7, the sprouts will be ready to feed. This method is preferred for sprouting larger quantities of seeds.

Kiddie Pool Method:
Growing sprouts in a kiddie pool is a great way to provide fresh greens for your chickens on-site and at a larger scale. Pick a location that the chickens have access to, if there is not good soil, add topsoil to the area. Spread the grain/seeds out in layer across the soil you don't want them piled on top of each other—wheat or sunflower seeds work best for this method. Water the seeds thoroughly and place the kiddie pool, face down, over the seeds. Water the seeds daily to keep them moist. After a few days, you should start to see sprouts appearing, once the sprouts have grown a few inches tall (usually after about 7-10 days) then they're ready to be devoured. *Alternate option:* grow the sprouts inside of the Kiddie-pool instead of underneath it. Ethier way is fine.

The Tray Method

The Kiddie Pool Method

| 7.1 Avoiding Harmful Foods & Plants | 7.2 Recognizing Potential Hazards | 7.3 The Importance of Regular Monitoring & Helpful Charts |

CHAPTER 7 SAFETY PRECAUTIONS & BEST PRACTICES

In this chapter, we will explore the essential safety measures required to maintain the health and well-being of your chickens. We will discuss potential dietary dangers, hazards to avoid, and the importance of regular observation.

7.1 Avoiding Harmful Foods and Plants

While chickens are known for their ability to eat a wide variety of foods, it's important to note that not all foods or plants are safe for them. Certain substances can be toxic to chickens, causing harm to their health and, in some cases, leading to severe illness or even death. Therefore, it's crucial to be aware of what your chickens are consuming and ensure that their diet is both nutritious and safe. If your flock free ranges during the day, then it would be worth while to make sure that theyre are none of the plants listed below in their unrestricted areas.

Harmful Foods

1. Chocolate: contains theobromine (and caffeine), substances that are toxic to many animals, including chickens. It can cause heart problems and, in large amounts, can be fatal.

2. Avocado: The skin and pit of an avocado contain persin, a fungicidal toxin that can cause heart problems and respiratory distress in birds.

3. Onions: contain thiosulphate, which can cause anemia in chickens by destroying their red blood cells. **Garlic contains this compound also but is only toxic in very large amounts.

4. Caffeine: found in coffee, tea, and energy drinks, can overstimulate a chicken's nervous system, leading to heart problems and potentially death.

5. Alcohol: can cause liver and brain damage in chickens, just as it can in humans. It can also lead to dehydration and poor egg production.

6. *Green* Tomatoes or *Green* Potatoes: The green parts of these plants, including the leaves and stems, contain solanine, a toxic substance that can cause problems with the nervous system and digestive tract.

7. Processed Foods: Although it might be tempting to throw the leftover frozen pizza into the run, I would not. And here's why; Feeding chickens processed or factory-made foods is discouraged due to their lack of essential nutrients and the presence of potentially harmful preservatives and additives, which can also cause digestive issues in chickens. Furthermore, processed foods are typically high in salt and sugar. A diet of fresh, natural foods is the best way to ensure your chickens' health and well-being.

Harmful Plants

8. **Rhubarb**: The leaves contain oxalic acid, which can cause kidney damage in chickens.

9. **Foxglove and Nightshades:** These plants are highly toxic and can cause heart problems, seizures, and even death in chickens.

10. **Rhododendrons and Azaleas** (which are in the same plant family): They contain a toxin called in their leaves, flowers, and nectar. If ingested, this toxin can affect a chicken's nervous system, leading to symptoms such as drooling, digestive upset, loss of appetite, diarrhea, depression, weakness, loss of coordination, and a weak heart rate. In severe cases, it can even be fatal.

11. **Lilies:** Many types of lilies, including tiger lilies, Easter lilies, and daylilies, are toxic to chickens. They can cause symptoms such as lethargy, depression, vomiting, inappetence, tremors, seizures, and even kidney or liver failure.

12. **Oleander:** All parts of the oleander plant are toxic to chickens. Ingestion can cause digestive upset, heart function problems, and even death.

13. **Castor Bean:** The seeds of the castor bean plant contain ricin, a highly toxic compound. Ingestion can lead to abdominal pain, drooling, vomiting, diarrhea, excessive thirst, weakness, and loss of appetite.

14. **Daffodils:** (not to be confused with Dandelions) The bulbs of daffodils are toxic to chickens. They can cause severe stomach upset, convulsions, and a serious drop in blood pressure.

Remember these lists are not exhaustive, when in doubt, it's best to err on the side of caution and avoid feeding your chickens anything that could potentially harm them. Always provide a balanced diet of safe, nutritious foods to ensure their health and well-being.

DUTTON & CASEY

These beautiful Easter Egger Brothers live on Sanity Ranch and share the responsibility of their flock equally.

7.2 Recognizing and Avoiding Potential Hazards

In maintaining the health of your chickens, it's crucial to recognize and avoid potential hazards. Below is a list of commonly overlooked or underestimated consumption hazards:

Moldy food: can produce harmful mycotoxins, which can cause a range of health problems in chickens, including respiratory distress, digestive problems, and reduced egg production—**even before the mold is visible** to the naked eye. Keep foods dry, check feeders frequently for mold growth, and turn over bedding materials.

Pesticides: can be harmful to humans and chickens alike, so to ensure that any fruits, vegetables, or herbs you provide are free from these, buy organic or wash them well before serving.

Home Treatments: Medications and/or supplements do not always interchange freely between humans and various pets or varied livestock; they should only be given under the guidance of a veterinarian.

Toxic Flora: As mentioned, be aware of any toxic plants or fungus in your garden and the surrounding areas that your birds have access too. Install fencing or poultry netting where needed.

Food Composition: Avoid feeding your chickens any foods or items that are stringy and sticky (like potato skins) or easily compacted when wet. A great example is large amounts of bread, which can clog up or impact the bird's crop once it reverts back to a doughy mixture. Breads can also be full of yeast, which can lead to Sour Crop. Another example of a stringy food that is commonly missed as a hazard is pre-cut/pulled grass. In Nature, chickens peck at grass and retrieve small pieces at time, however pre-cut grass in their run can and will be consumed at lengths and could cause impaction.

Food-drawn Predation and Pest: Chickens can fall prey to various predators; such as, foxes, raccoons, coyotes, and hawks. Secure housing, enclosed chicken runs, and monitored free ranging are some of your best defenses, however, proper food management is crucial. Do not leave food out overnight, or nearby in trashcans, as it can attract predators (or it can attract rodents that draw in predators). Consider using feeders specifically constructed to manage and distribute food safely and effectively.

7.3 The Importance of Regular Monitoring and Observation

Regularly monitoring your chickens' behavior and health is a critical aspect of their care. Any seemingly innocuous changes in appetite, behavior, or appearance should be noted and can be the difference between life and death, or effective home remedies and expensive vet bills. We have provided you with a few charts that demonstrate normal and healthy appearances.

The following are a few infographics that you can use as guidelines.
(*These and more can be printed out from Sanityranch.com*)

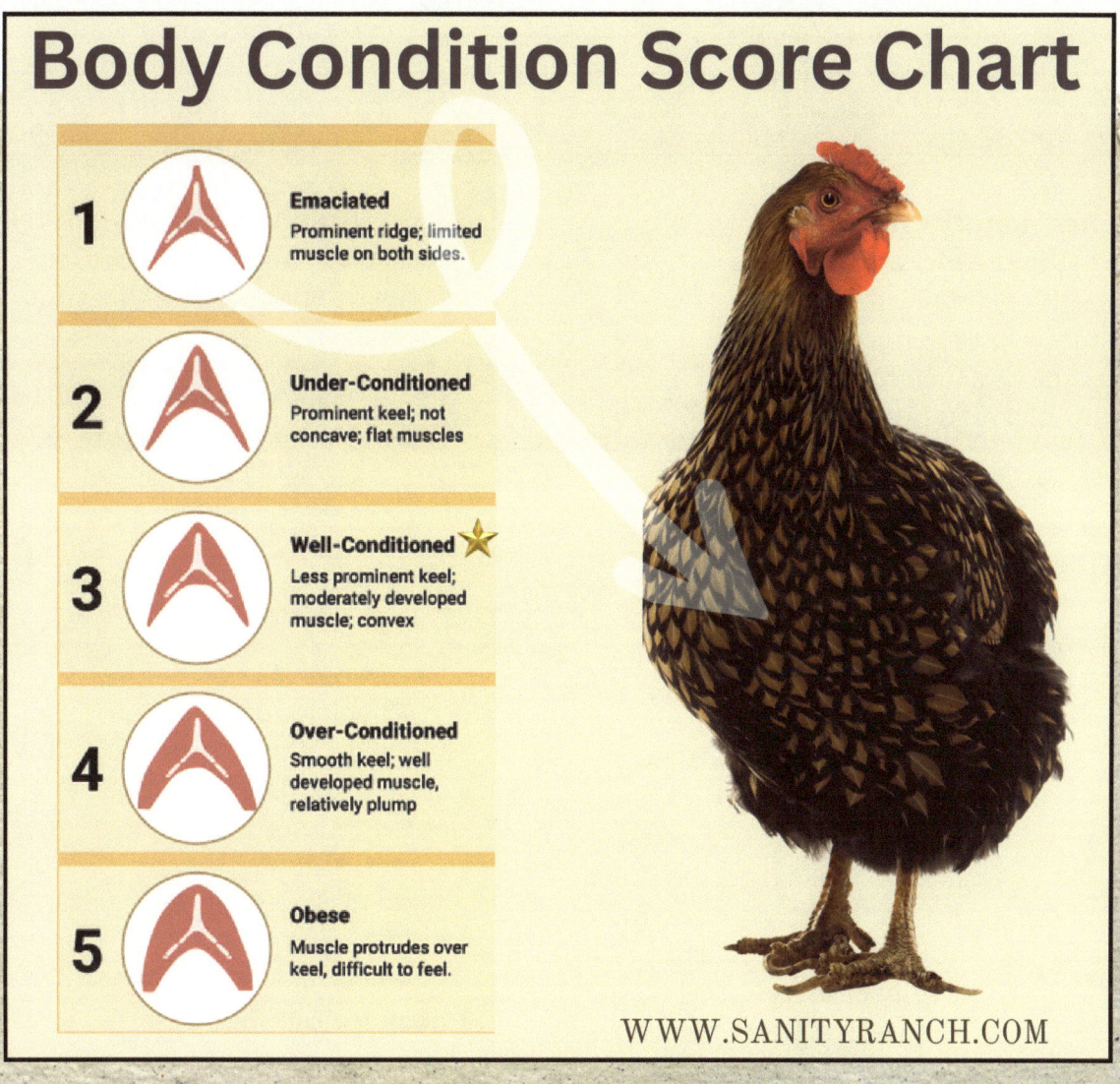

MONTHLY CHICKEN 10-PT Checkup

1. General Observation
Behavior: Chickens should be alert and active. Lethargy or isolation from the flock can be a sign of illness.
Posture: A healthy chicken stands upright. Hunching or drooping wings can indicate discomfort or sickness.

2. Feathers
Condition: Feathers should be smooth and well-preened. Broken, missing, or ruffled feathers can indicate mites, lice, or over-mating.
Molting: Chickens naturally lose and regrow feathers. Ensure it's a regular molt

3. Vent Area
Cleanliness: The vent should be clean without fecal buildup.
Discharge: There shouldn't be any discharge or signs of diarrhea.

4. Skin and Legs
Skin: Check for parasites, redness, or inflammation.
Legs and Feet: Ensure they are smooth without scales lifting (a sign of scaly leg mites).

Check for bumblefoot (swollen foot or limping).

5. Comb and Wattles
Color: A bright red comb and wattles are usually a sign of good health in most breeds. Pale or bluish combs can indicate poor circulation or respiratory issues.
Texture and Size: Check for swelling, lumps, or scabs.

6. Crop
Fullness: The crop should be full in the evening (after eating) and empty or nearly empty in the morning. A hard or swollen crop can indicate an impacted crop.

7. Respiratory Check
Breathing: Chickens should breathe quietly without wheezing, gasping, gurgling or coughing, which may be signs of a respiratory issue.

8. Beak and Nostrils
Beak: Ensure the beak is not overgrown or cracked. **Nostrils:** They should be clear without any discharge. Discharge can be a sign of a respiratory infection.

9. Eyes
Eyes should be clear and bright. Cloudiness, discharge, or swelling can be signs of an infection or injury. Bulging or discoloration, can be a sign of Mareks.

10. Parasites
External: Check for lice, mites, and ticks.
Internal: Look out for signs of worms in their droppings.

WWW.SANITYRANCH.COM

Hen Anatomy

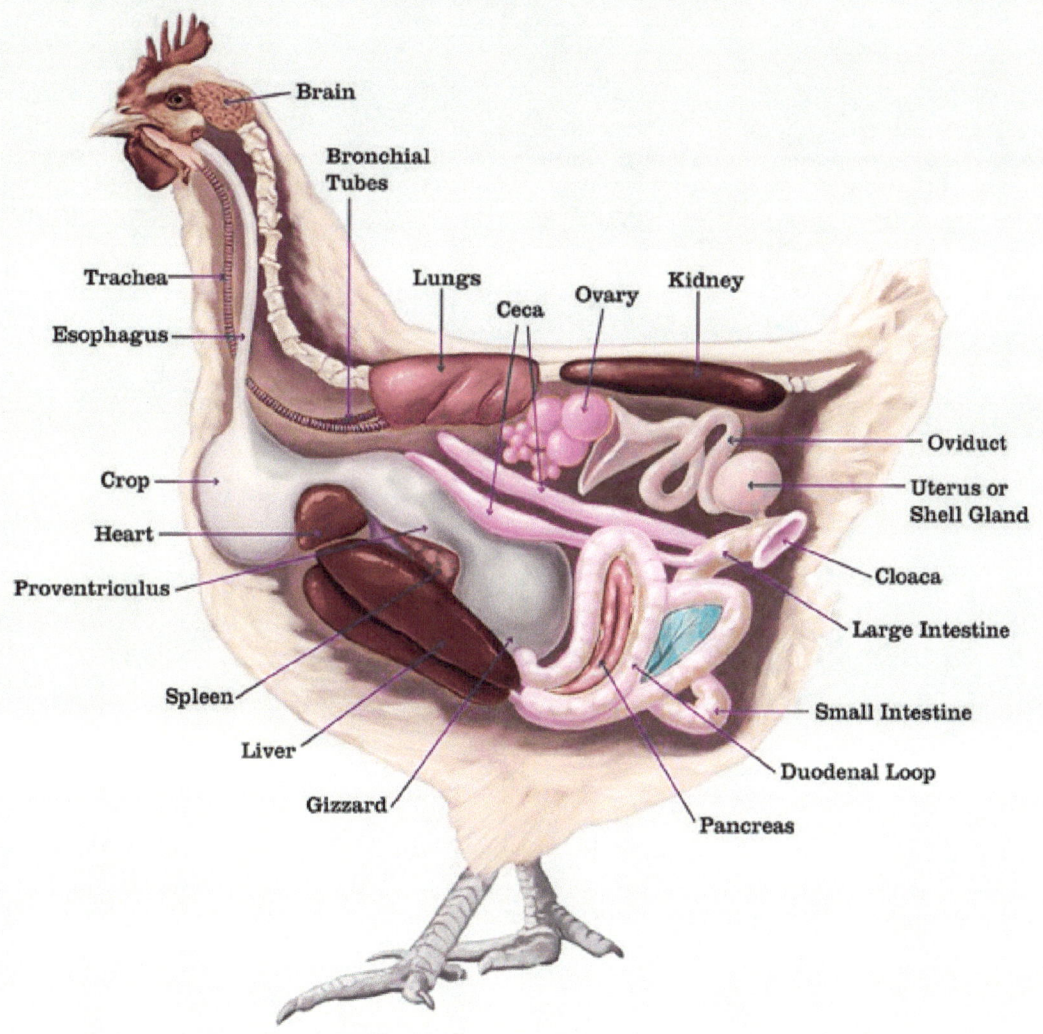

By adhering to these guidelines, and familiarizing yourself with these charts, you can support the safety and health of your chickens, while also providing them with a diet that supports their well-being and protects them from potential harm. Responsible feeding and care are crucial aspects of their well-being, allowing them to live happy, healthy lives.

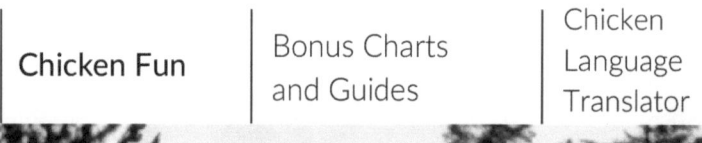

| Chicken Fun | Bonus Charts and Guides | Chicken Language Translator |

CHAPTER 8
THE CHICKEN KEEPER'S TREASURE TROVE

Welcome to this special bonus chapter, where the unexpected meets the indispensable! As seasoned chicken keepers know, the journey with our feathered friends is filled with delightful surprises and invaluable lessons. Here, we've curated a unique collection of tidbits, from whimsical anecdotes and trivia to hands-on tips and tricks that every chicken enthusiast will find invaluable. So, fluff up your nest, settle in, and let's dig in!

Ha Ha Ha Ha Ha Ha Ha

Jokes:

1. Why did the chicken go to the séance?
   - To get to the other side!

2. Why did the chicken sit on her eggs?
   - B/c she was tired of "laying" them!

3. Why did the chicken cross the playground?
   - To get to the other slide!

4. Why did the rooster join a gym?
   - He wanted to work on its "pecks"!

5. Why are chickens so awesome?
   - just BECAWWWWWWs.

Did You Know !

Chickens are quite communicative and we have over 30 distinct vocalizations cataloged; all convey different messages, from alerting the flock about a nearby predator to expressing contentment.

Dinosaur Descendants: Chickens, along with other birds, are the closest living relatives to dinosaurs. In fact, studies on the T. rex's proteins have shown that this mighty dinosaur shares more in common with modern chickens than with reptiles. So, every time you look at a chicken, you're getting a tiny glimpse into the prehistoric past!

Just like humans, chickens experience REM (Rapid Eye Movement) sleep, which means they can dream. If you've ever noticed a chicken twitching or making soft noises while resting, they might be in the middle of a dream!

The domestic chicken we know today is a descendant of the red junglefowl from Southeast Asia. Historical records suggest that chickens were domesticated over 8,000 years ago!

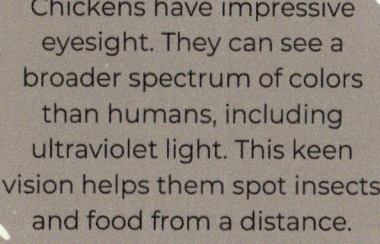

Chickens have impressive eyesight. They can see a broader spectrum of colors than humans, including ultraviolet light. This keen vision helps them spot insects and food from a distance.

NAME THAT BREED!

1. Silkie 2. Rhode Island Red 3. Lace Wyandotte 4. Legbar 5. Easter Egger 6. Marans

*MEMBERS OF THE NIGHTSHADE FAMILY, SUCH AS TOMATOES AND PEPPERS, SHOULDN'T BE CONSUMED BY YOUR FLOCK WHEN THEY'RE UNDER-RIPE. ADDITIONALLY, THE LEAVES AND STEMS OF THESE PLANTS ARE TOXIC AND SHOULD BE AVOIDED.

EAT THIS, NOT THAT
CHICKEN EDITION

OKAY AS A TREAT
- GREEK YOGURT
- SCRAMBLED EGGS
- RICE AND COOKED PASTA
- MEAL WORMS
- NUTS

GOOD *not an exhaustive list
- LEAFY GREENS
- SPROUTS
- VEGETABLES
- FRUITS
- HERBS

BAD
- ANY PART OF AN AVOCADO
- ONIONS
- PROCESSED FOODS
- UNCOOKED BEANS
- PITS
- CANDY OR REFINED SUGAR
- MOLDY FOODS OR FEED
- POTATO SKINS

WWW.SANITYRANCH.COM

YEARLY CHORE CHART

JAN
- Check for frostbite
-
-
-

FEB
- Prepare for spring molting
- plan for chicks!
-
-

MARCH
-
- Clean and disinfect coop
-
-

APRIL
- Plant chicken-garden plants
- Check for external parasites
-
-

MAY
- trim toenails / crossbeaks
- keep an eye out for broodiness
-
-

JUNE
- Monitor for signs of heat stress
- add electrolytes to water
-
-

JULY
-
- Monitor for signs of heat stress
- Limit treats to cool fruits
- High predator alert

AUGUST
-
- Monitor for signs of heat stress
- Limit treats to cool fruits
-

NOTES:

FILL IN AND CUSTOMIZE TO YOUR FLOCK

SEP
- Prepare for fall molting
- Harvest chicken garden plants
- secure coop vulnerabilities
-

OCT
- Check for internal parasites
- Winterize coop
-
-

NOV
- limit free ranging-high predator risk
-
-
-

DEC
- Conduct an end-of-year health check
- Insulate coop with extra bedding
-
-

DAILY
- collect eggs
- check feeder/water
-
-

WEEKLY
- turn over bedding
-
-
-

MONTHLY
- 10PT Monthly Checkup
-
-
-

TASKS FOR
-
-
-
-

NOTES:

Print-out at WWW.SANITYRANCH.COM

1. Walk your property and pick the location. Choose a spot that gets sun approx. 6-8 hours a day for your chicken garden. Map out its dimensions.

_____ X _____

2. Circle options from these chicken-safe plants, or use the index in the back of this book:

Herbs:

- Mint: Repels insects and rodents.
- Basil: Boosts the immune system.
- Oregano: Acts as a natural antibiotic.
- Lavender: Repels insects and has calming properties.
- Thyme: Good for respiratory health.
- Rosemary: Repels insects.
- Parsley: High in vitamins.
- Lemon Balm: Calming and repels insects.
- Dill: Aids in digestion.
- Cilantro/Coriander: Good for digestion.

Vegetables:

- Leafy Greens: A favorite treat for chickens. (ie, Kale: High in nutrients.)
- Cabbage: Hang in the coop for enrichment.
- Cucumbers: Refreshing and hydrating.
- Squash: Both the vegetable and the seeds.
- Carrots: Including the tops.
- Broccoli: Both the heads and leaves.
- Peas: Chickens love pecking at pea plants.

Flowers:

- Marigolds: Repels pests and can be used to darken yolks.
- Nasturtium: Both flowers and leaves are edible; also acts as an antiparasite
- Sunflowers: Chickens love the seeds.
- Calendula: Petals can be used to darken yolks.
- Echinacea: Boosts the immune system.

Grains:

- Corn: Can be grown for chickens to peck at.
- Wheat: Can be grown and harvested for feed.
- Oats: Can be grown and used as part of their diet.
- Barley: Good for sprouting!.

Fruits:

- Strawberries: Chickens can eat both the berries and the plants.
- Blueberries: High in antioxidants.
- Raspberries: Can eat both the berries and the leaves.
- Melons: Chickens love both melon flesh and seeds.

3. Research the ideal planting dates for each type of plant in your zone, and make a planting schedule for each one; write the planting dates (pd) and harvest dates (hd) next to each selected plant.

You can visit https://planthardiness.ars.usda.gov to find your zones and dates.

4. Play with your garden layout on the next few pages, taking into account the spacing requirements of each plant. Be sure to assign a length to each sq. unit and write it on the top of the page.

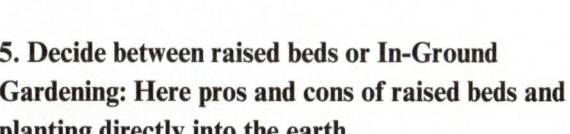

5. Decide between raised beds or In-Ground Gardening: Here pros and cons of raised beds and planting directly into the earth.

Raised Bed Gardening:
Pros:
- Better Soil Control
- Improved Drainage
- Fewer Weeds
- Easier on the Back
- Pest Control
- Extended Growing Season
- Prevents Soil Compaction

In-Ground Gardening
Pros:
- Natural Soil Web: Directly planting into the earth allows plants to tap into the natural soil ecosystem,
including beneficial microbes and fungi.
- Deep Root Growth: Plants can extend their roots deeper into the ground, accessing more nutrients and water.
- Less Initial Cost: No need for building materials or large amounts of soil mix.
- Natural Moisture Retention: In-ground gardens often retain moisture better than raised beds.
- Larger Planting Area: You can easily expand an in-ground garden without the constraints of bed borders.

Cons:
- Initial Cost: Building or buying raised beds and filling them with soil can be more expensive initially.
- More Frequent Watering: Raised beds can dry out faster than in-ground gardens, especially in hot weather.
- Limited Root Depth: Some plants with deep root systems might be restricted.

Cons:
- Weed Growth: More susceptible to weeds growing amongst your plants.
- Soil Quality: You're at the mercy of your native soil, which might not be ideal for all plants.
- Pest and Disease Vulnerability: More exposure to soil-borne diseases and pests like moles or groundhogs.
- Harder on the Body: Bending down to ground level can be tough on the back and knees.
- Potential for Soil Compaction: Walking on the garden can compact the soil, which can hinder plant root growth.

CHICKEN TRANSLATOR

CASUAL CONVERSATION
SOFT, REPETITIVE SOUNDS THAT CHICKENS MAKE WHEN THEY'RE CONTENT AND EXPLORING THEIR SURROUNDINGS.
THEY UTILIZE INFLECTIONS AND PATTERNS TO INFER DIFFERENT MEANINGS WITHIN SIMILAR PHONETICS, A TECHNIQUE THAT HAS BEEN LOOSELY COMPARED TO THE COMPLEXITY AND INTELLIGENCE OF MANDARIN!

THE BROODY GROWL
A LOW SHRILL, WARNING SOUND THAT A BROODY HEN MAKES WHEN SOMEONE APPROACHES HER NEST. IT'S HER WAY OF SAYING *"STAY AWAY FROM MY EGGS,"* AND YOU'LL KNOW IT WHEN YOU HEAR IT!

CALCKILING OR THE EGG SONG
A SERIES OF LOUD, EXCITED CLUCKS THAT A HEN MAKES AFTER LAYING AN EGG. IT'S VERY LOUD!! THOUGHT TO BE A WAY OF DRAWING ATTENTION AWAY FROM THE NEST AS WELL AS LETTING THE ROOSTER KNOW THAT SHE IS READY TO BE ESCORTED BACK TO THE FLOCK. WHICH IN THE WILD CAN BE QUITE FAR!
THE ROOSTER ANSWERS THIS CALL WITH A UNIQUE, BUT SIMILAR, VOCALIZATION OF HIS OWN.

COMPLAINING
A TROUBLING SOUND HENS MAKE WHEN THEY HAVE TO LAY AN EGG AND THE NEST ISN'T READILY AVAILABLE, NEW LAYERS WILL MAKE THIS NOISE MOST OFTEN.

CROWING
THE LOUD, PROUD CALL THAT ROOSTERS ARE KNOWN FOR. THEY CROW TO ASSERT THEIR DOMINANCE, WARN OTHERS, OR JUST TO SAY *"HELLO, IT'S ME, IM SPEAKING!"*. IT CAN ALSO BE USED TO ROUND UP THEIR HENS, AND IN OTHER SCENARIOS. THE DIFFERENCE IN MEANING IS REFLECTED IN SUBTLE CHANGES IN THE SOUNDS, OR INFLECTION.

- EVERY ROO'S CROW IS UNIQUE TO THEM

CHICKEN
TRANSLATOR

PURRING
A soft, rolling sound that chickens make when they're relaxed and content, similar to a cat's purr. Typically when they feel safe, and especially after a fright. *"OH THANK YOU, HOLD ME, LOVE ME"*

TRILLING
A gentle low, quiet, & tri-repetitive sound, that chicks, make when they're settling down to sleep or rest this is where the purr is thought to originate. *"THIS IS NICE"*

DISTRESS CHIRP
A high-pitched, urgent sound that chicks make when they're in distress. *"HELP I'M COLD, OR BEING HELD CAPTIVE, OR LOST!"*

"SONAR" PEEPS
The soft, high-pitched sound that baby chicks make. They chirp to communicate with their mother and their siblings. *"HEY MOM? HI MOM, MOM, LOOK MOM, IM OVER HERE MOM."*

ALARM/SQUAWK
A series of short, sharp sounds that chickens make when they spot a predator. The sound varies depending on whether the threat is from the air or the ground, and if it is approaching. *"THAT'S SUSPICIOUS- OKAY VERY SUS!" "OMG, THEY'RE COMING FOR THE EGGS!"* This can begin as a low growl

TID BITTING
A series of quick little tuks that a hen makes to her chicks or rooster makes when they've found food. It's their way of telling the rest of the flock *"LOOK WHAT I'VE FOUND! COME AND GET IT."*

WWW.SANITYRANCH.COM

Recipe Index

Bold Recipes signify that they can be enjoyed by the flock AND your family.

Although, you probably want to add some salt or sugar to the dish *after* you have separated the portion going to your flock.

If it's a baked good then you would do this before cooking and make two versions, but dont forget to mark them so you dont get them mixed up !

R.1 Basic Homemade feed p.8
R.21 Autumn Apples p.55
R.23 Acorn Squash Pie p.57
R.33 ACV tincture p.75
R.37 Boredom Buster Blocks p.81
R.31 Breath Easy Fried Rice p.70
R.32 Broccoli Sprouts Quiche DF p.73
R.30 Calming Spray p.69
R.24 Christmas Cookies for Santa Caws p.58
R.12 Coop Comfort Double-Oatmeal p.43
R.15 Cucumber Salad p.49
R.28 Crustless Spice Pie p.67
R.16 EE Crunch p.50
R.40 ER Tonic p.88
R.39 Extreme Heat. p.85.
R.26 Fancy Feather Fish Tacos p.65
R.19 Fruit Kabobs p.53
R.29 Go Bananas Bites p.68
R.44 Healthy Birthday Cake p.96
R.11 Hearty Vegetable Stew p.41
R.35 Immune Boost-Broth p.78
R.6 Melon Medley p.25
R.36 Meatloaf for Irritated Chickens p.79
R.41 Mealworm Popsicles p.93
R.17 May Muffins p.51
R.9 OMG Harvest p.35
R.43 O-mega Tuna Party p.95
R.25 Omega-3 Power Snacks p.64
R.2 Overachiever, The p.10
R.14 Pink Oat Balls p. 48
R.8 R&R Nesting Box Mix p.31
R.38 Recipes for Extreme Cold p.89

R.42 Scramble Egg Surprise, p.94.
R.5 Spring-Greens Salad p.23
R.45 Sprouts: Jar Method p. 101-102
R.47 Sprouts: Kiddle Pool Method p.101
R.46 Sprouts: Tray Method p.101, 103
R.7 Summer Berry Blast p.29
R.18 Summer Squash Casserole p.52
R.3 Supplemental Salad p.13
R.34 Swinging Head O' Cabbage p.77
R.22 Trick or Treats p.56
R.4 Vegetable Mashup p.15
R.27 Whole-Egg Veggie Bake p.66
R.20 Watermelon Splash p.54

Ingredient-Benefit Index
(In Alphabetical Order)

Benefit Index by Ingredient

A

Aloe Vera: When given in moderation, the gel can support digestive health and act as a detoxifier. It's also known for its soothing and healing properties when applied to minor cuts or skin irritations.

Alfalfa: provides chickens with essential proteins, amino acids, and vitamins, supporting feather growth, egg production, and overall health. Its high xanthophylls which can also enhance the yellow color of egg yolks.

Almonds: provide chickens with a boost of protein and essential fatty acids, supporting muscle growth and feather health. However, they should be given in moderation as an occasional treat.

Anise: This herb can stimulate appetite and help with digestion. Its licorice-like flavor can be appealing to chickens and can mask the taste of medicines or supplements.

Apples: provide chickens with essential vitamins and fiber, supporting their overall health and aiding digestion, while also offering a tasty, low-calorie treat. However, it's vital to avoid giving them apple seeds, which contain small amounts of cyanide.

Apple Cider Vinegar: Often used in small amounts in chicken water, it can act as a natural probiotic, supporting gut health and can help with the condition known as Sour Crop.

Arugula: Nutrient-dense leafy green that can provide a variety of health benefits for chickens. It's high in vitamins A, C, and K, as well as calcium and potassium. These nutrients can support overall health, boost the immune system, and contribute to strong bones and eggshells.

B

Bananas: Rich in potassium. Supports heart and kidney health.

Barley: Good source of energy. High in fiber and nutrients.

Basil: contains vitamins A and K, as well as antioxidants. It's believed to have anti-inflammatory and antibacterial properties. For chickens, basil is thought to promote mucus membrane health, which can be beneficial for respiratory health.

Bee Balm: aids in respiratory and digestive health. Scattering bee balm in your nesting boxes can be calming to hens and also act as an antiseptic and antibacterial agent.

Blackberries: are loaded with fiber, vitamins, antioxidants, and manganese, support bone development and immune health

Blueberries: Rich in iron, zinc, fiber, vitamin C, and vitamin K, help chickens combat stress and disease. The leaves of the bush are also safe to eat and offer high antioxidant content

Broccoli: High in vitamins A, C, and K. Supports overall health.

Butter Lettuce: a good source of vitamins A and K, and also provides some vitamin C and folate. It's a hydrating and low-calorie treat that chickens generally enjoy. Like other leafy greens, it should be fed in moderation as part of a balanced diet.

Butternut Squash: Rich in vitamins A and C, both of which are essential for immune health. It also contains fiber, potassium, and magnesium. The seeds of butternut squash are often used as a natural dewormer for chickens.

C

Cabbage: A great source of hydration with vitamins and minerals; can be hung in the coop for pecking entertainment/boredom/enrichment.

Calendula: Can enhance the color of egg yolks, and has anti-inflammatory properties.

Chamomile: Calming herb, can help reduce stress. Also thought to have antimicrobial properties.

Carrots: A great source of vitamins, particularly vitamin A, which is essential for optimal eye health and immune function in chickens. They also contain fiber, which aids in digestion.

Cayenne pepper/Capsaicin: Believed to increase blood circulation and can help warm chickens in winter. Also has anecdotal evidence to support parasite moderation.

Cherries: Rich in antioxidants. Can improve immunity.

Cherry Tomatoes: They're high in acid and provide a variety of nutrients, including vitamins A and C, potassium, and lycopene. Lycopene is an antioxidant that can help protect against cellular damage. **it's important to note that tomatoes should be fed to chickens in moderation and the green parts (leaves, stems, and unripe fruit) should be avoided as they contain solanine, which can be toxic to chickens.

Chervil: Believed to support respiratory health. High in vitamins C and A.

Chia seeds: High in omega-3 fatty acids, beneficial for feather and skin health.

Chicory: Supports digestion and can improve liver health.

Cinnamon: Can support respiratory health.

Corn: Good source of fast energy. High in carbohydrates.

Cranberries: contain a type of compound called proanthocyanidins (PACs). PACs are believed to inhibit certain harmful bacteria, including E. coli, from adhering to the urinary tract in humans. Some preliminary research on chickens and other poultry has indicated that cranberry extracts might have similar effects in these animals, potentially reducing the levels of E. coli and other harmful bacteria in their digestive systems.

Cucumber: Hydrating and cooling. Can be a refreshing treat.

D
Dandelion Greens: High in calcium, vitamins A, C, and K. Good for bone and immune health.

Diatomaceous Earth: It is believed that DE is a natural antiparasite when added to the feed and a pest control aid when sprinkled in and around the coop. However, while many chicken keepers swear by the benefits of DE, there is limited scientific research to support some of these claims.

Dill: This herb has antioxidant properties and can promote respiratory health.

E
Echinacea: Stimulates the immune system, helping to fight off disease.

Elderflower: This can be a natural remedy for respiratory issues in chickens.

Eggs: Full of protein and can be fed back to hens, but they should be cooked to prevent them from developing a taste for raw eggs.

Egg Shells: provide a natural source of calcium.

F
Fennel: Believed to improve laying and egg quality.

Flaxseeds: are known to increase the omega-3 content in eggs laid by hens that consume them. They are considered a superfood and can contribute to the production of healthier chicks.

Flowers (edible varieties): Many flowers, like marigolds and nasturtiums, can provide a range of nutrients. See Flowers in the following Index.

G

Garlic: Natural antimicrobial. Good for immune health.

Ginger: Known for its anti-inflammatory properties and can aid in digestion.

Goldenrod: This herb is thought to have anti-inflammatory properties.

Grains (e.g., oats, wheat): Good source of energy. High in fiber and nutrients.

Grapes: A tasty treat in moderation, but should always be given seedless and chopped to prevent choking.

Green beans: A source of vitamins and minerals, they should be cooked or chopped to make them easier to digest.

H

Hemp seeds: High in omega-3 and omega-6 fatty acids, and a good protein source.

Hibiscus flowers: Can act as a cooling agent and are rich in antioxidants.

I

Insects: A natural source of protein, essential for egg production and muscle growth.

K

Kale: High in vitamins K, A, and C. Good for overall health.

Kelp Meal: Rich in iodine and also contains potassium, magnesium, calcium, and iron.

Kiwi: High in vitamin C and a source of antioxidants, though should be given in moderation.

L

Lavender: Calming herb, may help reduce stress in chickens. It's especially beneficial to broody hens who don't get up and move around like they should.

Leafy Greens: (I.e. kale, spinach, and Swiss chard) They're are high in vitamins A, C, K, and minerals such as iron and calcium. They can boost the immune system and overall health of chickens.

Lemon Balm: A calming herb that may help reduce stress and has some antibacterial properties. It also repels certain bugs.

Lentils: a great source of protein and also contain fiber, iron, and B vitamins.

Linseed (Flaxseed): A source of omega-3 fatty acids that can promote shiny feathers and overall health.

M

Marigolds: The petals are believed to enhance the color of egg yolks when included in a chicken's diet. They contain xanthophylls, a type of pigment that contributes to the yellow-orange color in egg yolks. Marigolds also have antioxidant properties and can help to deter insects.

Mealworms: High in protein. Good for feather and egg health.

Melon: Hydrating and cooling treat. High in vitamins A and C.

Millet: A nutritious grain that provides a good source of protein, good for feather growth and egg production. It also contains B vitamins for energy. Additionally, millet is a favorite among chickens due to its small, easy-to-peck size.

Mint: known for its cooling and calming effects. It's also a good source of vitamins A and C, as well as iron and manganese. For chickens, mint is often used for its natural insect-repelling properties. It's also thought to help lower body temperature, which can be beneficial in hot weather.

N

Nasturtiums: rich in vitamin C and have natural antibiotic properties. Some chicken keepers believe that nasturtiums can help to deter pests, such as lice and mites. The flowers, leaves, and seeds of the nasturtium plant are all safe for chickens to eat.

Nettle: High in calcium, can boost eggshell strength. Also supports feather health.

O

Oats: high in fiber and provide a good balance of carbohydrates and protein. They also contain essential minerals like manganese, selenium, and zinc.

Oregano: known for its antibacterial and antiviral properties, which can help support the immune system. It's also a good source of vitamins K and E, calcium, and antioxidants. It is currently being studied as a natural antibiotic in many commercial poultry farms. Oregano can help your chickens combat E.coli, coccidiosis, salmonella, and avian flu by strengthening their immune systems.

P

Parsley: rich in vitamins A, C, and K, as well as iron and antioxidants. It's believed to support the immune system and promote overall health. It's also thought to aid in egg production.

Peaches: (Do not feed pits) Good source of vitamins A and C. Supports immune health.

Pears: High in fiber. Good for digestion.

Peas: good source of protein and contain a variety of vitamins and minerals, including vitamin A, vitamin C, iron, and zinc.

Pumpkin: are rich in vitamins A, C, potassium, and zinc, supporting overall health. Some chicken owners use pumpkin seeds for their potential natural deworming properties, courtesy of the cucurbitacin compound.

Q
Quinoa: High in protein. Good for muscle development.

R
Raspberries: aid digestion, bolster the immune system, stabilize blood sugars, and promote heart health.

Rice: Easy to digest. Can be a good source of energy.

Rosemary: High in antioxidants and believed to support respiratory health.

S
Sage: Antioxidant-rich and thought to support general health and it is known to combat salmonella. Can be fed free-choice or dried in their feed.

Spinach: High in vitamins A, K, and iron. Good for bone health and egg production-Though best given in moderation due to its oxalic acid content.

Strawberries: High in vitamin C and antioxidants. Good for immune health

Sunflower seeds: High in healthy fats and proteins, which are essential for feather growth and overall health. They also contain significant amounts of vitamin E and selenium.

Sweet potatoes: Provide essential nutrients when cooked.

Swiss chard: A good source of vitamins A, C, and K, as well as magnesium, potassium, and iron. These nutrients can support overall health, boost the immune system, and contribute to strong bones and eggshells. Swiss chard can also provide fiber, which can aid in digestion.

T

Thyme: High in antioxidants. Supports respiratory health.

Tomatoes: They're high in acid and provide a variety of nutrients, including vitamins A and C, potassium, and lycopene. Lycopene is an antioxidant that can help protect against cellular damage. **It's important to note that tomatoes should be fed to chickens in moderation and the green parts (leaves, stems, and unripe fruit) should be avoided as they contain solanine, which can be toxic to chickens.

Turmeric: Anti-inflammatory. Can support overall health.

W

Watercress: Packed with vitamins and minerals, it's a nutrient-rich green for poultry.

Watermelon: Hydrating treat. High in vitamins A and C.

Wheat: A common grain that provides energy and essential nutrients.

Woundwort (Stachys): Thought to have antiseptic properties.

Y

Yarrow: This herb can act as a natural astringent and may help in blood clotting. It's also believed to have anti-inflammatory properties.

Yogurt: A source of probiotics, yogurt can support gut health. However, it should be given in moderation and without added sugars or flavors.

Yucca: Some believe yucca can help reduce odor in chicken droppings due to its saponin content.

Z

Zucchini: A good source of water content, which can help keep chickens hydrated. It also contains vitamins C and B6, potassium, and magnesium.

Quick-Pick Reference Guide
(By Category)

Quick-Pick Ingredient List (by category)
*not an exhaustive list.

Fruits
Apples: High in fiber and vitamin C. Provides hydration and a refreshing treat.
Bananas: Rich in potassium. Supports heart and kidney health.
Blueberries: High in antioxidants, vitamins, and minerals. Good for immune health.
Cherries: Rich in antioxidants. Can improve immunity.
Melon: Hydrating and cooling treat. High in vitamins A and C.
Peaches: (Do not feed pits) Good source of vitamins A and C. Supports immune health.
Pears: High in fiber. Good for digestion.
Strawberries: High in vitamin C and antioxidants. Good for immune health.
Watermelon: Hydrating treat. High in vitamins A and C.

Vegetables
Broccoli: High in vitamins A, C, and K. Supports overall health.
Carrots: High in vitamins A and K. Good for vision and immune health.
Corn: Good source of energy. High in carbohydrates.
Cucumber: Hydrating and cooling. Can be a refreshing treat.
Leafy Greens (ie Kale): High in vitamins K, A, and C. Good for overall health.
Peas: High in protein and fiber. Good for digestion and muscle health.
Pumpkin: High in vitamins A and C. Seeds can help with parasite control.
Spinach: High in vitamins A, K, and iron. Good for bone health and egg production.
Sweet potatoes: High in vitamins A, C, and fiber. Supports digestive health & immune system.

Grains
Barley: Good source of energy. High in fiber and nutrients.
Corn: Good source of energy. High in carbohydrates.
Oats: Good source of energy. High in fiber and nutrients.
Quinoa: High in protein. Good for muscle development.
Rice: Easy to digest. Can be a good source of energy.
Wheat: Good source of energy. High in fiber and nutrients.

Nuts and Seeds
Almonds (crushed): High in protein and healthy fats.
Flaxseeds: High in Omega-3 fatty acids. Good for feather health and egg quality.
Peanuts: High in protein and healthy fats.
Pumpkin seeds: Some believe that they can help with parasite control.
Sunflower seeds: High in healthy fats and protein. Good for energy and muscle development.

Proteins
Eggs: High in protein. Eggshells provide a natural source of calcium.
Lentils: High in protein. Good for muscle development.
Mealworms: High in protein. Good for feather and egg health.
Peas: High in protein and fiber. Good for digestion and muscle health.
Soybeans: High in protein. Good for feather and egg health.

Herbs
Basil: Antioxidant-rich. Supports mucus membrane health.
Garlic: Natural antimicrobial. Good for immune health.
Oregano: Natural antimicrobial. Good for respiratory and immune health.
Parsley: High in vitamins A, C, and K. Supports overall health and may boost egg production.
Thyme: High in antioxidants. Supports respiratory health.

Flowers
Calendula: This can enhance the color of egg yolks.
Marigolds: High in antioxidants. Can support skin health and enhance the color of egg yolks.
Nasturtiums: Natural antibiotic. Can support immune health.
Sunflowers: The seeds are high in healthy fats and protein. Good for energy and muscle development.

Spices
Cayenne pepper: Believed to increase blood circulation and can help warm chickens in winter.
Cinnamon: Can support respiratory health.
Turmeric: Anti-inflammatory. Can support overall health.

Glossary

Important Terms

Bantam: A miniature chicken, often one-fourth to one-fifth the size of standard chicken breeds.

Broody: A hen that wants to hatch eggs and starts sitting on them consistently.

Candling: The process of shining a light through an egg to check its development.

Clutch: A group of eggs laid by a hen in consecutive days, typically she will wait until she has 8-12 to set them.

Cockerel: A young male chicken less than one year old.

Comb: The fleshy crest on the top of a chicken's head.

Crop: A pouch at the base of a chicken's neck where food is stored before digestion.

Dust Bathing: A behavior where chickens roll in dust* to clean their feathers.

Free Range: Chickens that are allowed to roam outside during the day.

Hen: A mature female chicken.

Incubation: The process of keeping eggs warm to allow them to develop and hatch. Above 90 degrees for development to begin, but 99.5-100.5 for healthy development. See printable hatching chart at sanityranch.com for more details on hatching.

Layer: A hen that is raised primarily for egg production.

Molt: The process where chickens shed old feathers and grow new ones.

Nest Box: A designated place in the coop where hens lay their eggs.

Pecking Order: The social hierarchy among a flock of chickens. This is always evolving and can get complicated.

Pullet: A young female chicken less than one year old.

Roost: A bar or plank where chickens perch to sleep.

Rooster: A mature male chicken.

Vent: The external opening for a chicken's intestinal, urinary, and reproductive tracts.

Wattles: The fleshy lobes that hang down on either side of a chicken's beak.

Grit: Small rocks or pebbles chickens need eat to help grind down food in their gizzard.

Gizzard: A part of a chicken's stomach that grinds food using grit.

Hackles: The feathers around a chicken's neck, that can be used to determine gender
.

Pin Feathers: New feather growth on a chicken.

Sexing: Determining the gender of chicks.

Sex-Linked: Chicks born with physical traits that tell the gender.

Straight Run: Chicks that are sold without being sexed.

Tractor: A movable chicken coop without a floor, allowing chickens to forage on fresh ground and stay protected.

Setting: When a broody hen sits on eggs to incubate them. This begins development in eggs.

ABOUT US

Hello!

Thank you for your interest in our book! We hope you enjoy it as much as we enjoyed creating it. Eva and I met because of our shared love of Silkies, a very special breed of chickens. Our respective talents and personalities alined to create this project. My background is rooted in the world of biological and veterinary sciences. I've had the privilege of interning at the Atlanta Zoo, the Atlanta Aquarium, Georgia Southern's Raptor Center, as well as other various local animal shelters. However, my passion for literature and writing led me down a different path than my schooling would have suggested. After several years of working as a vet assistant, I decided to pursue writing full-time. My history has positioned me to weave my love for animals and nature into my work. Beyond being an author, I am a dedicated homesteader and an advocate for sustainability. Alongside my husband, I run Sanity Ranch, a haven for animals (and people) in need of peace and tranquility. Our ranch is more than just a home—it's a testament to our commitment to humanitarianism and sustainable living.

with love,
N.J. Simat

Hi!

Before I dived deep into the crazy world of chicken breeding, I served my community as a police officer, a role that instilled in me a deep sense of responsibility, commitment, and patience-which are all attributes necessary to care for these wonderful creatures! I'm also a mother to two charismatic and compassionate children, and a wife to a perfectly wonderful husband. Family is the most important thing in my life and I've always been passionate about creating a nurturing home environment. This same passion extended beyond my human family when, five years ago, I began breeding Silkies. These charming and fluffy creatures have since become a significant part of our world. Now, I'm thrilled to share my experience and love for backyard chickens with you through this cookbook.

with love,
Eva Carver

Acknowledgements

First and foremost, we extend our heartfelt gratitude to our chickens. Without their daily antics, unique personalities, and the joy they bring into our lives, this book would not have been possible. They have been the true inspiration behind every page, and for that, we are so grateful!

To our families, you've generously shared our time, allowing us to immerse ourselves in this work. Your encouragement and belief in our vision are invaluable. We are deeply thankful for every sacrifice made and every moment spent cheering us on from the sidelines.

And finally to our readers, this book is as much yours as it is ours. Thank you for believing in us and encouraging us to continue to create.

Please Share Your Recipe Photos from "#TheCoopbook"

We love to see your twists on the recipes & reading your comments means the world to us!

Let's spread the love for backyard chickens together!

If you've enjoyed "The Coopbook" and found value in its pages, we'd be incredibly grateful if you could take a moment to leave a review on Amazon or Google.

Your insights inspire us to continue creating content that serves our wonderful community.
We create to care for our animals.

Connect with Us!

For a chance to connect with the breeder and author, follow us on Instagram: **@SilkieAcres and @NJSIMAT**
We want to hear your thoughts, questions, and concerns: we're all here to learn and grow together!

More Titles from N.J. Simat:

Fiction
Club Daze and The Subtle Realm www.clubdazebook.com
Astral Academy and The Subtle Realm
www.AstralAcademyBook.com

Nonfiction
Backyard Chickens Coloring Journal
The Coopbook

About The Publisher

Canary Agency is the "mom and pop shop" of publishing. We believe in the artists retaining their rights to their work and only serve to assist in the process in an a-la-cart, services-led format, from start to finish. We help bring stories to life with unparalleled passion and dedication. Our commitment to nurturing new voices and crafting great stories is evident in every title we champion. Discover a world where every author feels like family at [www.canaryagency.com]

www.ingramcontent.com/pod-product-compliance
Lightning Source LLC
Chambersburg PA
CBHW040715220426
43209CB00091B/1840